CONFLICT

Causes and Cures

by
MIKE SMITH

Jacksonville College

JACKSONVILLE COLLEGE BOOKSTORE

ATHLETIC DEPT. BOOK

Copyright © 2014 by MIKE SMITH

CONFLICT
CAUSES AND CURES
by MIKE SMITH

Printed in the United States of America

ISBN 9781629522326

All rights reserved solely by the author. The author guarantees all contents are original and do not infringe upon the legal rights of any other person or work. No part of this book may be reproduced in any form without the permission of the author. The views expressed in this book are not necessarily those of the publisher.

Unless otherwise indicated, Bible quotations are taken from The King James Version: *The Hebrew-Greek Key Study Bible-KJV*. Copyright © 1984 by Spiros Zodhiates, AMG Publishers (Chattanooga, Tenn.).

www.xulonpress.com

Dedication

*To my wife Susan,
who is the ornament of a
meek and quiet spirit,
which in the
sight of God
is of great price.*

Contents

Dedication v
Foreword ix
Acknowledgements xi
Introduction xiii
Section 1 ..... Principles of Conflict xv
    Introduction 17
        Chapter 1-Sentence Definitions of Conflict 19
        Chapter 2-Scars from Conflict 25
        Chapter 3-Sure Truths about Conflict 31
        Chapter 4-Signs of Conflict 35
        Chapter 5-Structural Levels of Conflict 40
        Chapter 6-Styles of Conflict Management 47
        Chapter 7-Generational Differences 54
    Summary of Section 1 57
Section 2 ..... Problems (Causes of Conflict) 59
    Introduction 61
        Conflict 10-Worship Wars 66
        Conflict 9-Church Polity 75
        Conflict 8-Staff 81
        Conflict 7-Sexual Immorality 89
        Conflict 6-Incompetence 97
        Conflict 5-Church: Conflicted/Dysfunctional 103
        Conflict 4-Communication 110
        Conflict 3-Change 118
        Conflict 2-Leadership Too Strong/
        Leadership Too Weak 128

      Conflict 1-Control/Power 136
   Summary of Section 2 147
Section 3..... Possibilities (Cures for Conflict) 149
   Introduction 151
      Chapter 1-Education 154
      Chapter 2-Mediation 160
      Chapter 3-Restoration 171
   Summary of Section 3 177
Conclusion 179
Appendix A 181
Appendix B 183
Appendix C 185
Appendix D 188
End Notes (by section) 190
References 197

Foreword

Psalm 133:1 says, "Behold how good and how pleasant it is for brethren to dwell together in unity." Jesus prayed for unity among believers as recorded in John 17. We are truly doing the Lord's work when we seek to bring peace.

It has been my privilege to work with Mike Smith at the Southern Baptists of Texas Convention. Daily, during Mike's time at the SBTC, he dealt with conflict. Mike's training, educational credentials, and assignments all related to helping people resolve conflict. His heartbeat for the people of God is evident. He is a man who epitomizes a peacemaker.

This book is divided into three primary sections. The first section is about general issues related to conflict. Signs of conflict may not be readily visible; there are often underlying problems that go undetected at first. Mike helps you look beneath the surface to see potential flashpoints. Scars from conflicts heal slowly; scars from prior difficulties can become raw once again. Knowing the personality types provides a context for understanding how people act and react. The DISC evaluation is highlighted as a preferred method of determining a person's personality proclivities.

The second section of the book delves into the types of conflicts that arise in the church. Music seems to have been one of the major causes for disruption of fellowship in congregations over the past twenty years. Leadership styles or the lack of leadership altogether can result in discontent. Power struggles for control often create tensions that spill over into open hostilities. One of the greatest challenges for a congregation is to be open to change. Demographics in the neighborhood or unhelpful church traditions may be positive or negative motivators for change, respectively. Getting a pliable mindset to adopt change is outlined in this chapter.

Section three is a microcosm of the book as it relates to the common elements for addressing conflict. The lead chapter in section three begins with the theological underpinnings necessary to confront a spiritual problem. Scripture is the basis for education in church conflict resolution. Chapter two shows the practical application of the role for the mediator in conflict. The last chapter illustrates how restoration is possible when conflict causes a temporary suspension of ministry.

Conflict—Causes and Cures is a tool to bring people together. Mike's down-home style sets you at ease. "Grandchildren's word" introduces you to the subject in most chapters. Inside you will find scholarly references and insightful analysis. I encourage you to make this a reference when conflict arises. "Live peaceably with men," Romans 12:18.

Dr. Jim Richards
Executive Director
Southern Baptists of Texas Convention
December 17, 2013

Acknowledgements

Conflict: Causes and Cures is the compilation of academic and practical experiences gathered from the laboratory of my life across these past 44-plus years, 17 years of which were spent pastoring Baptist churches. I served as Director of Missions in West Texas for seven years and in East Texas for 14 years. The 150 churches in these associations provided weekly opportunities for conflict management.

Following my 21-year tenure as a Director of Missions, I joined the Southern Baptists of Texas Convention staff as Director of the Minister and Church Relations Department. This position allowed me to work with more than 2,000 churches. I served as a confidant who listened, cried, and prayed with pastors experiencing conflict. I was a coach who advised church leaders on how to walk through conflict. I served as a consultant who directed churches in the midst of conflict.

Now as president of Jacksonville College, I have many opportunities to practice my conflict management skills with the students, faculty, accreditation and regulatory organizations. I am grateful for the training I received from such conflict management experts as Speed Leas, Ken Sande, Richard Blackmon, Nancy Ferrell, George Bullard, Norris Smith, Larry Savage, Marlin Thomas, Blake and Ken Coffee, Lifeway Christian Resources, the North American Mission Board, and many others.

I appreciate those churches, deacons, individual associations, state conventions, and the Texas Association of Directors of Missions, all of which invited me to hold Conflict Management Seminars and to serve as a consultant.

Acknowledgements

I have served in over 3,000 conflict cases. The case studies I share in this book are real, with the names changed and the stories altered to protect the confidentiality of those involved.

I am indebted to my wife, who allowed me to pursue my Ph.D. with my dissertation in the area of conflict. She shared our time together and accepted the interruptions of phone calls from hurting pastors and damaged churches at all hours.

I am thankful to Ann Cumbee, my Ministry Assistant, for typing this manuscript and for proofreaders, Marolyn Welch and Vanita Pettey. I am grateful to Danny Morris for the graphic artwork. Danny formatted the cartoons that my pastor friend Bob Reid drew for me. I have included the cartoons and stories about my grandchildren to provide a bit of humor. In conflict, everyone needs to laugh at times to keep from crying. I am also thankful for the Trustees of Jacksonville College because they encouraged me to write and publish this book. All proceeds from this work will go to the ministry of Jacksonville College.

I still have much to learn. Conflict resolution is not a science, but an art. I did not choose this direction for my life; God placed me in situations that have given me opportunities to become equipped and to help equip others in the area of conflict resolution.

To God be the Glory,
Mike Smith, Ph.D.
President of Jacksonville College
Philippians 1:21

Introduction

Conflict is serious and needs the church's serious attention. Personally, I have caused conflict, suffered from conflict, and helped mediate conflict. In doing so, I have gleaned a vast amount of knowledge in this area during my 44 years in the ministry.

My intention for this book is to share the principles of conflict, to share the top ten causes of conflict within churches and to examine the practices of conflict resolution. My goal for you as you read this book is that you would desire to be an active peacemaker.

The Bible is clear in admonishing believers to be in unity with one another.

> Matthew 5:9 – "Blessed are the peacemakers: for they shall be called the children of God."
>
> Matthew 5:25 – "Agree with thine adversary quickly, whiles thou art in the way with him; lest at any time the adversary deliver thee to the judge, and the judge deliver thee to the officer, and thou be cast into prison."
>
> Matthew 18:15 – "Moreover if thy brother shall trespass against thee, go and tell him his fault between thee and him alone: if he shall hear thee, thou hast gained thy brother."
>
> II Corinthians 5:18 – "And all things are of God, who hath reconciled us to himself by Jesus Christ, and hath given to us the ministry of reconciliation."

My prayer is that every church will have a group of members—whether it is the deacons, church staff, or lay persons—who will become equipped with the skills of conflict mediation in this book. At the end of every chapter, a learning activity can be done individually or in a class setting. Anyone who wishes to teach conflict resolution more extensively may contact me for the slide presentation that may be used to accompany this study.

I am available to come to churches and teach on conflict management. The three most popular teaching formats are

1. one-hour overview of conflict.
2. Saturday morning 9:00 a.m.-12:00 noon. (This is popular with deacon groups.)
3. Sunday through Wednesday evenings for 1.5 hours each evening.

I am also available to consult with churches currently in conflict. The format of consultation depends upon the church's conflict. Sometimes the situation necessitates a more formal arena where I serve as a mediator with the two conflicted parties. I will serve as a moderator for a business meeting. I will conduct a church-wide analysis and make recommendations as a consultant. I come to a church only by invitation of the pastor and/or leadership.

Read *Conflict: Causes and Cures*, and if God sparks a desire for more in this area, contact me.

Mike Smith
Jacksonville College
105 B. J. Albritton Drive
Jacksonville, TX 75766
msmith@jacksonville-college.edu
903-721-0279

Section 1
Principles of Conflict

Introduction

Principles are fundamental truths or methods of operation.[1] Conflict Management is more of an art than a science. By this, I mean that conflict management is more caught than taught. There are some basic observations, but much of conflict management is best learned from experience. Even so, some fundamental truths must be accepted and appreciated in order to serve skillfully as a conflict mediator.

Grandchild Story
(East Texas Accent)

When our granddaughter, Emma, was three she was watching her mother and our daughter, Martha Elaine, work on a bicycle. Martha Elaine asked her son William to go get a <u>wrench</u> for her. Emma, who is a biblical Martha like her mother, said, "I can get it," and quickly left. When she returned, she handed her mother a bottle of <u>Ranch</u> dressing.

Chapter 1

Sentence Definitions of Conflict

What is Conflict?

Definition: Conflict comes from the Latin word *comfligere*, which refers to an "act of striking together."[1] Striking a match against a matchbox produces a fire. Some people have such a clashing personality that the moment they walk into a room, conflict erupts; comments like "Everything was peaceful until you walked into the room" aptly describe them.

It was my first time to attend a meeting in a particular association. I felt uneasy from the beginning because of my newness in the organization. My discomfort increased as the meeting proceeded. Every item brought for discussion before this deliberating body met with vocal resistance from one man. He was quick to his feet, loud in speech, angry, and rude in his presentation. I had never witnessed such hostility and resistance to such common items of discussion. On the other hand, everyone else was positive and agreeable.

When the moderator called for the vote, this man opposed every item brought before the body. After the meeting adjourned, I asked some of the leaders who the man was and why he was so disagreeable. They all laughed, and someone said, "That's John. He is an *a-gin-er*. He always votes against everything we discuss."

"But he's so loud and rude," I responded.

They laughed again and said, "That's just John."

What I thought was a major conflict, they accepted as common, everyday action. This taught me that not everyone defines conflict the same way.

(The rest of the story: The next year I asked the nominating committee to make that man the clerk. He had to spend his time writing. He did not have time to voice opposition.)

Definition: Conflict is a situation in which two or more human beings desire goals that are attainable by one or the other, not by both.[2] The following exemplifies conflict arising from a common, desired goal.

Only one could be elected class president. Every effort was exerted by both candidates to attain the position. What started as a friendly campaign soon turned ugly and vindictive as both sought the office. Though once best friends, the desire to be class president turned them into arch enemies. Conflict has a way of being divisive.

Definition: Conflict is a power struggle over differences. This could be differing information, beliefs, interest, desires, or values.[3]

Today, when the subject of conflict is discussed, the phrase *power struggle* is used more than any other descriptive term. When groups of people spend time together, power struggles soon surface. Ten years of surveys reveal that power struggles continue to be the number one cause of conflict. This topic will be discussed in detail in later chapters.

Definition: Conflict is when two or more objects try to occupy the same space at the same time.[4]

If I, weighing over 400 pounds, am sitting in a chair and someone else comes in to sit in the same chair at the same time, there will be a conflict either with the other person, the chair, or me! We vividly see this problem when two children are playing and each one wants the same toy. Since only one can have the toy, hair pulling or biting usually occurs as conflict erupts.

The proverbial "beauty is in the eye of the beholder" applies to every conflict. In response to what one person would describe as severe conflict, another would shrug and say, "That's just everyday life." Therefore, whether much or little is made of conflict depends on the person.

Two Ways to Look at Conflict

Ken Sande in *The Peace Maker* has a chapter entitled "Is This Really worth Fighting Over?" Sande suggests as you view a conflict, ask yourself, "Do I have a sensitive attitude or a sinful behavior?"[5] In most conflicts, it would be wise not to be so sensitive.

Sensitive

A college student sat across from my desk and asked permission to share on a personal level. I agreed to listen and help if I could. She related the following incident. A student in the cafeteria had said something about her to a friend without knowing whether the information was true. Then her friend asked her if she was going to confront the person who had said these things. At this point, she asked for my advice. I asked if she was offended or hurt by what was said. She assured me such talk did not bother her. I told her that she had two choices. The first choice was to confront the person who talked about her publicly; the second choice was to overlook what was said.

The incident with the college student reminds us that overlooking offenses is the right thing to do under two conditions.

1. when the offense has not created a wall between you and the other person or caused you to feel differently toward him or her
2. when the offense has not caused serious harm to God's reputation, to others or to the offender[6]

Sometimes, the best way to resolve conflict is to simply overlook the offense. Numerous Bible passages speak of this.

> Proverbs 10:12 - "Hatred stirreth up strifes: but love covereth all sins."
> Proverbs 12:16 - "A fool's wrath is presently known: but a prudent man covereth shame."
> Proverbs 15:18 - "A wrathful man stirreth up strife: but he that is slow to anger appeaseth strife."
> Proverbs 17:9 - "He that covereth a transgression seeketh love; but he that repeateth a matter separateth very friends."
> Proverbs 17:14 - "The beginning of strife is as when one letteth out water: therefore leave off contention, before it be meddled with."
> Proverbs 19:11 - "The discretion of a man deferreth his anger; and it is his glory to pass over a transgression."
> Proverbs 20:3 - "It is an honour for a man to cease from strife: but every fool will be meddling"
> Proverbs 26:17 - "You grab a mad dog by the ears when you butt into a quarrel that's none of your business." (The Message)
> "He that passeth by, and meddleth with strife belonging not to him, is like one that taketh a dog by the ears."
> Ephesians 4:32 - "And be ye kind one to another, tenderhearted, forgiving one another, even as God for Christ's sake hath forgiven you."
> Colossians 3:13 - "Forbearing one another, and forgiving one another, if any man has a quarrel against any: even as Christ forgave you, so also do ye."
> 1 Peter 4:8 - "And above all things have fervent charity among yourselves: for charity shall cover the multitude of sins."

Overlooking an offense is not an act of denial as in a passive process but a deliberate, active choice because of God's work of grace in you. You deliberately choose not to talk about it, dwell on it, or allow yourself to become bitter.

The truth of the matter is that too many are too sensitive. Too many "wear their feelings on their sleeves" and are easily hurt. As a Christian, you need to mature and grow in grace so as not to be so sensitive. When you face a conflict, ask, "Am I being too sensitive?"

Sinful Behavior

The second question each person must ask himself before confronting others is, "Is there sinful behavior in my life?" Jesus said as much or more in Matthew 7:3-5.

> And why beholdest thou the mote that is in thy brother's eye, but considerest not the beam that is in thine own eye? Or how wilt thou say to thy brother, Let me pull out the mote out of thine eye; and, behold, a beam is in thine own eye? Thou hypocrite, first cast out the beam out of thine own eye; and then shalt thou see clearly to cast out the mote out of thy brother's eye.

Before confronting others about *their* sins, ask:

1. Am I guilty of any unconfessed sin?
2. Am I guilty of not submitting to authority?
3. Am I guilty of mistreating others?
4. Am I guilty of lust of the flesh, pride, love of money, or fear of others?
5. Am I guilty of breaking my word or not fulfilling all my responsibilities?

If there is sinful behavior, then repent and confess.[7]

More times than I want to admit, I have been quick to see sin in others only to be convicted of the same sin in my life. Before confronting others, I find it is always good to stop and let the Holy Spirit reveal any unconfessed sin in my own life.

Learning Activity

1. Write your definition of conflict.

2. After reading the definitions of conflict in this chapter, has your definition of conflict changed in any way? Explain.

3. What verse from the provided verses in this chapter speaks to you and why?

4. Share an offense you have overlooked.

Chapter 2

Scars from Conflict

Tabernacle Baptist Church on Plum Creek was the first church to be served by a 19-year-old Brown University student with much zeal but very little experience. It all began when a notice posted on a bulletin board outside his professor's office caught his attention.

"Wanted! Baptist Preacher - Apply inside."

With fearful excitement, he opened the door. Dr. Jones explained that this church was 50 miles from the campus and needed a preacher. The student left his name, dorm room number, and campus phone number with the professor. He left the office and walked across campus, wondering if he would ever get an opportunity to preach. As he entered his dorm room, the phone was ringing. He quickly answered it and was surprised to hear, "I am Bill White, Deacon of Tabernacle Baptist Church. Can you preach for us this Sunday?" The student answered, "Yes," without giving it any thought.

He preached that Sunday and was invited back the second Sunday to preach again. This young man was one of three candidates that the church was considering. The third Sunday he preached, they called him as their pastor. He set about to grow the church. Every weekend, he would leave campus and go to the church field to visit on Saturdays and preach on Sundays. The church started growing with several new people attending.

The church was having an "Ole Fashioned Brush Arbor Revival" when after the service, two men grabbed the young pastor's arms and took him outside. They let him know that if he brought any more "lake trash" to the church, they would see to it he never preached again. As he walked away, a woman came up and swung her purse at him as she screamed, "Don't you ever bring those dirty, barefooted "lake trash" into this church again!"

The young pastor left emotionally scarred and fell asleep that night crying and praying. Thoughts of never going back to the church entered his mind, even though other members of the church began to call and come by to encourage him to stay and not to give up.

Remember the woman who said, "Don't you ever bring those dirty, barefooted "lake trash" into this church"? A few years later, her daughter was walking along a major highway and had a bad accident that resulted in the amputation of her foot.

The Psalmist warns in Psalm 105:15, "Touch not mine anointed, and do my prophets no harm." The Bible is filled with examples of those who have been hurt by conflict. There are at least 133 cases of conflicts recorded in the scriptures.[1]

Examples of Conflict in the Old Testament

Genesis 3:1-19 identifies five areas of conflict:

Conflict between the word of God and Satan (v. 1-5)
Conflict within as a result of sin (v. 6-7)
Conflict between man and God (v. 8-10)
Conflict between man and his spouse (v. 11-13)
Conflict within the ordered structure (v. 14-19)

Genesis 4:1-16 Conflict between brothers—sibling rivalry conflicts
Genesis 13:5-10 Conflict over land, soil

Examples of Conflict in the New Testament

Matthew 4:1-11 Conflict between Jesus and Satan
Mark 3:1-6 Conflict between Jesus and Pharisees over traditions
Acts 6:1-4 Conflict between church members over fairness in being served
Acts 15:1-19 Conflict over doctrinal stance
Acts 15:36-41 Conflict over personnel service
Galatians 2:11-21 Conflict between two saints—Peter and Paul

Examples of Conflict in Baptist History

On May 8, 1845, the Southern Baptist Convention was formed out of conflict with the Triennial Convention when their mission society said a slave owner could not be appointed as a missionary.[2]

In 1900, the Baptist Missionary Association of Texas was formed out of a conflict within the Baptist General Convention of Texas.[3]

On May 25, 1950, The Baptist Missionary Association of America (known as the North American Baptist Association until 1969) was formed from a conflict within the American Baptist Association.[4]

November 10, 1998, the Southern Baptists of Texas Convention was formed out of conflict within the Baptist General Convention of Texas over several issues, one being inerrancy of scripture.[5]

Examples of Conflict in Baptist Life Today

In 1986, there were 88 pastor terminations per month in the Southern Baptist Convention

In 1996, there were 117 pastor terminations per month in the SBC.

In 2013, there were 100 pastor terminations per month in the SBC.

In summary, that is 1200 terminations a year, 100 terminations a month, 3 terminations a day, and 1 termination every 8 hours.[6]

The chart below depicts what is happening to ministers because of conflict.[7]

Reasons	Clergy	General Population
Burnout	15%	10%
Divorce	15%	40%
Chemical Dependence	5%	11%
Mental Disorders	2%	10%
Immorality	10%	15%

The percentage of pastors who leave the ministry because of stress is 40%. Forty years ago, insurance actuarial tables indicated pastors were one of the safest groups to insure because of good physical and mental health. Today, they are considered one of the highest risk groups.[8]

The chart below depicts the results of church conflicts.[9]

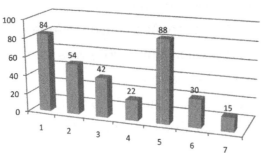

Legend

1. Members who left the church
2. Members who withheld tithes and offerings
3. Lay leaders who resigned
4. Programs or activities that were stopped
5. Pastors who left/had to leave
6. Staff members who left/had to leave
7. Churches that split/members that started a new church

Learning Activity

Write or share something you have experienced personally from a conflict that has caused a scar during your ministry or in the ministry of someone you know.

Grandchild Story
(R-rated Annuity)

Susan and I were keeping the grandchildren for a week while their parents served as sponsors at a church camp. We tried to do different outings each day to keep them entertained, so we decided to take them to see a movie. To make sure that the feature was age appropriate, Susan got her I-pad and began to read the descriptions of all the available movies. She read aloud one review that indicated nudity in the film and said, "We can't go to that one. It has nudity." Later, when my older grandson, William, asked about the same movie, our seven-year-old grandson, Jacob, said, "No, we can't see that one. It has annuity."

Chapter 3

Sure Truths about Conflict

Conflict exists.

To deny that conflict exists is a result of either having your head in the sand or lying to yourself. At the weekly pastors conference, a pastor who had recently experienced a conflict shared his hurts with the group. The pastors listened and offered words of encouragement and prayers. One particular pastor always remarked, "I have a good church, and we never have conflict." However, in his fifth year of pastoring that church, conflict that he had denied erupted. To deny conflict only delays its destructive damage.

Conflict is neither inherently good nor inherently evil.

How conflict is managed determines if it is good or bad. While I was attending Southern Seminary, I had a roommate from China. He shared with me the significance of the two Chinese characters for the word *crisis*.

One character represents danger; the other character represents opportunity. This is the truth in every conflict. While danger exists, the opportunity to do well exists also. Looked at another way, conflict is like a dollar bill, which is an inanimate object. A dollar bill is neither good nor evil. How the dollar bill is used determines the potential for good or evil.

Conflict can be healthy or unhealthy.

Conflict does not occur where there is apathy. Some churches that boast they never have conflict are often the churches where nothing is occurring. While I do not recommend this growth tactic, some pastors have shared with me that they intentionally try to keep a conflict in the church because it creates energy. Crowds gather where there is a fight. As I say around my house, "If we did not occasionally have conflict, Susan would never cut the grass."

Note the chart below.[1]

Healthy Conflict	Unhealthy Conflict
Dealt with directly in a biblical manner	Dealt with indirectly with emotion
Decides to glorify God	Decides to destroy others
Leads to deeper intimacy and trust	Leads to broken relationships
Develops mutual respect	Develops disrespect—name calling
Desires the good of the church	Desires personal gain—"I want my way."

Sure Truths about Conflict

Learning Activity

1. List the Sure Truths about conflict and share a personal experience to illustrate each Sure Truth.

2. Discuss the difference between healthy and unhealthy conflict.

Chapter 4

Signs of Conflict

Jesus' disciples followed him to the Mount of Olives and asked him, ". . .What shall be the sign of thy coming and the end of the world?" (Matthew 24:3). As the discussion proceeded, Jesus gave some signs that would enable men to recognize His return. Conflict often catches churches by surprise, but more often than not, there are already signs that indicate conflict. The following are a few of those signs.

Attendance and Offering

Several churches keep a "scoreboard" over the piano in the auditorium. This scoreboard records attendance and offering for that Sunday. People enter the sanctuary to worship, but quickly look at the scoreboard to see how many are in attendance compared to last week and a year ago. They evaluate the Sunday as good or bad based on the "nickels and noses" present.

A decline in attendance and offering may cause conflict or indicate that it is present. Commonly heard remarks might be, "Well, our preacher just isn't preaching like he used to;" "No one is visiting prospects like they should;" "I can remember when our church was full. Now there are only a few of us left." Some pastors take comments such as these very personally and start sending out resumes, believing it is time to move to another church.

Worship Services

Conflict may often be reflected in cold worship services. People do not sing with spirit and enthusiasm when in conflict. Jesus is clear that we cannot worship effectively when we have conflict. "Therefore if thou bring thy gift to the altar, and there rememberest that thy brother hath ought against thee; leave there thy gift before the altar, and go thy way; first be reconciled to thy brother, and then come and offer thy gift" (Matthew 5:23-24).

Refusal to Serve

When the church is in unity, everyone wants to serve. When the church is in conflict, it is difficult to find people to serve. In good times, people ask, "Pastor, what can I do to help?" In times of conflict, people are quick to say "No" when asked to teach or serve on a committee.

Low Level of Trust

Conflict breeds distrust. Everyone becomes suspicious of one another. People question every remark in a negative frame of mind.

Discordant Business Meetings

When a church is in conflict, the business meetings serve as an opportunity to air frustrations and anger. People who usually do not participate in the church business meetings may be present in an attempt to be heard and promote their agenda. The length of the business meeting often reveals the degree of conflict; the longer the meeting, the more intense the conflict. Some people attend every church service except the business meeting because of the reputation of church fights erupting during these meetings.

Body Language

Body language reveals much about a person's attitude. Conflict exists if the people who once hugged now avoid each other. Little groups that huddle in the church parking lot could also indicate the presence of conflict.

Increased Complaints

When complaints increase, conflicts are on the rise. People accuse the pastor of preaching at them. People openly share with the pastor that some of the members are upset with him. Some even boldly say, "It is time for you to resign."

Tribal Warfare

Every church averaging 100 or less in attendance has a *Tribal Chief, Bell Cow, Patriarch, Matriarch,* or *E. F. Hutton* (a well-known stockbroker), who is a person of influence. Conflict arises in a small church when the person of authority and influence is challenged. Often, the challenge comes from the pastor as he finds himself at odds with this leader over the decisions and direction of the church.

Personalities

A church of 100 will have 100 personalities. People see things differently. Some people have difficult personalities. People become hurt and angry if they interpret the rejection of their ideas as a rejection of themselves.

Change

Change inevitably leads to conflict. Change often creates a conflict not so much because of the issue itself but because of the way the leader introduces and manages the change.

The Top Ten Predictable Times for Conflict in a Church

1. Conflict is predictable during the Christmas and Easter seasons because it is a busy time and people are tired. There may be conflict between the pastor and the music leader.
2. Conflict is predictable during stewardship or budget promotion.
3. Conflict is predictable when adding staff.
4. Conflict is predictable during changes in the style of worship or organization.
5. Conflict is predictable during the pastor's absence, vacation, or mission trip.
6. Conflict is predictable during changes in the pastor's family. For example, when there is the birth of a child or when a pastor's child becomes wayward, remarks like, "He is spending too much time with his family," and "He cannot control his own household," are heard.
7. Conflict is predictable during generational change in the church, such as when there is an increase in young couples.
8. Conflict is predictable during the completion of a new building.
9. Conflict is predictable during a change in membership.
10. Conflict is predictable during the time between pastors.[1]

Signs of Conflict

Learning Activity

Get with someone and using the "Signs of Conflict," discuss the one that hurts the church the most.

Grandchild Story
(Dictionary Needed)

Logan, our number three grandchild, was riding in the car with my wife. Up to this point in his young life, the only way the word *accident* had been used was in relation to wetting his "pull-ups" or the bed.

As Susan carefully drove, a motorcyclist passed them at high speed. Susan spoke her thoughts out loud, "If he has an accident, he will die!"

Logan quickly replied, "Nonnie, how can he die from wetting his pants?"

Chapter 5

Structural Levels of Conflict

In the early 1980s, I had the privilege of attending a conference on conflict led by Speed Leas. Of all the conferences I have attended and books I have read, Ken Sande and Speed Leas have helped me the most in understanding conflict. One particular area that has been the most beneficial is the conflict levels found in Leas' book *Moving Your Church through Conflict*.[1] The following is a summary of his lecture, and more details can be found in his book.

Level 1   PROBLEM TO SOLVE

Issue: Real problems surface.
Language: Clear and specific - There can be misunderstandings and miscommunications, but more often, all sides understand the problem.
Objective: Solve the problem. At this stage, focus is on the problem, not the person.
Outcome: Win/Win - At this level, all parties involved can "win."
Strategy: Encourage participation by all persons involved. The use of collaborative problem solving is the best strategy.

Story (Part I): The deacons held their monthly meeting after the first Sunday evening service. After all the preliminary activity and reports, the chair asked if anyone had an issue to discuss. Bob quickly spoke up to say that the grass needed mowing. Several women had complained about the grass being higher than their ankles.

Jim responded, "Well, the lawn mower is broken."

Craig declared, "It is time we buy a new mower."

Level 2 DISAGREEMENT

Issue: Mixing of personalities, goals, values, or processes

Language: More vague and general - the phrase, "some say" is used. Hostile humor and put downs are used.

Objective: Self-protection is high. Everyone wants to fix the problem and come away looking good. There is a shift from problem-oriented to person-oriented. In level one, participants want to fix the problem, and in level two, they want to fix the person.

Outcome: Win/Win - It is still possible to find a solution wherein all sides "win."

Strategy: Continue to use collaborative problem solving, but maximize communication skills. The key is to define and discuss the issues, not personalities. Negotiation may be in order at this level.

Story (Part II): As soon as Craig declared that it was time to buy a new mower, Sam interrupted and interjected that a Snapper Mulcher/Mower was the best. Craig responded that a Sears Craftsman would do just fine.

Sam asked, "Why do some people in this church always think we have to buy the cheapest when my God owns the cattle on a thousand hills?"

Craig countered with, "Not all of us in this church have money growing on trees."

Level 3 CONTEST

Issue: The focus is on the person and not the issues. The focus shifts from self-protecting to winning.

Language: Often abrupt and curt - Over-generalizations often occur. "You always. . ." or "We never. . ." "You're trying to wreck this church when the majority does not agree with you" "They are going to break this church." Each side magnifies itself as good and the other side as bad. Sides are labeled with names such as *fundamentalist* or *liberal.*

Objective: Win, lose, or get my way.

Outcome: Win/Lose. Winning becomes an important objective. Resolution is possible, but rare.

Structural Levels of Conflict

Strategy: An outside third party mediator is suggested. The appeal is for the good of the church or organization. Personalities should be put aside and focus placed on the issues at hand.

Story (Part III): It was late. The chairman said that it was time to dismiss and deal with this problem later. The younger deacons gathered at the parking lot and voiced concerns that they felt the church needed to purchase a Snapper Mulcher/Mower.

Sam stated, "We can afford the best because God deserves our best."

The next morning at the Dairy Queen after a third cup of coffee, Craig said, "Men, if we don't watch it, these new young deacons are going to break this church. They do not know the value of a dollar."

Level 4 FIGHT/FLIGHT

Issue: Focus on issues shifts to focus on getting rid of the person with whom the problem is identified.
Language: Embellished - Scripture is often used to reinforce the argument. Words like "our *rights*" and "*our* church" are used.
Objective: To discredit the other side and win at all costs
Outcome: Lose/Leave - A church split, members leaving the church, or a physical fight could be the outcomes.
Strategy: Usually, the event is a business meeting. A vote is taken to indicate the numbers on each side of the issue. A third party, outside mediator who is viewed as part of the hierarchy or has influence helps.

Story (Part IV): The following month, the deacons meeting was short; emotions were high and anger prevailed. After a lengthy, heated debate over which brand of lawn mower to purchase, the deacons agreed to go to the business meeting and let the majority decide. Normally, a small group was present for Wednesday night business meetings, but this night the word had spread about the disagreement, and the house was full. Clearly, the sides were in place. The pastor had asked the Director of Missions to moderate. The Director asked that Christian decorum prevail.

Quickly, Sam rose and said, "I move we purchase a Snapper Mulcher/Mower for this church." Several voices give the "second" to the motion. The moderator asked for discussion.

Craig rose and said, "Director, you know me, and you know our church. We are just common, working-class people, and Sears products have always served us well. After all, the Bible says that we are to be stewards of God's money. The money we save on buying a Sears mower over the

Snapper mower could go to missions." The debate started, and both sides got emotional and threatened to leave the church.

Level 5 INTRACTABLE

Issue: Everything is out of control. Confusion reigns. The issue is lost, and the struggle is for power and control.

Language: Inflammatory language intensifies - Language that describes the other side as "of the devil," or "For the sake of the gospel, we must rid our church of these liberals" is often heard.

Objective: Destroy the other side. At this level, one side wants the other to suffer and hurt. Sometimes the one who suffers the most is the pastor.

Outcome: Lose/Lose - This level is unmanageable and out of control.

Strategy: Usually, someone will use the church's constitution to exert power and control. Sometimes, there is a need to bring in the police. Call for power to be enforced. This is war. Reason and rationalism have left at this level. The best hope is to take the vote and to let the majority rule, although this is not always the right conclusion. The minority side usually leaves, and the church could be hurt for years. However, in some cases, expelling the other side is best for the church.

Story (Part V): Craig rose for the fifth time and held in his hand the church's constitution and by-laws. He cited article eight that clearly stated the church will use the best stewardship principles in the Bible when purchasing property. He added, "This means we are bound by the by-laws to buy the Sears mower."

Sam shouted, "I am leaving. I do not want my family in a church with such little faith. We will go where God is honored and trusted." With that comment, he and his family walked out, along with five other families.

Structural Levels of Conflict

Levels of Conflict Chart

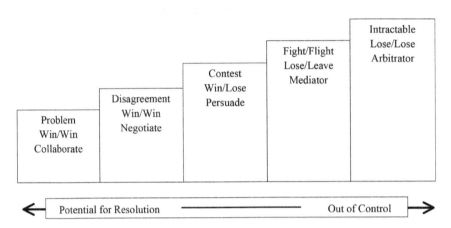

Structural Levels of Conflict

Learning Activity

From the column of Structural Level on the left, draw a line to the Language Indicator on the right that it matches.

Structural Level	Language Indicator
1. Problem to solve	a. We are not going to let them get their way. We've got to stand up for our rights.
2. Disagreement	c. This is a problem.
4. Contest	e. If the church votes for this, my family and I will be leaving.
6. Fight/Flight	g. The constitution clearly says this.
8. Intractable	i. I do not agree with you.

Grandchild Story
(Cold Awakening)

Our family enjoys a big bowl of Blue Bell Ice cream on a regular basis. The deep freeze works well, and often the ice cream is hard as bricks. As a result, Susan will sometimes put it in the microwave for a couple of minutes to thaw it out in order to make it easier to scoop.

Our grandson Logan's parents don't do this microwave routine before serving ice cream. Therefore, when he was visiting our house and saw his grandmother take the Blue Bell from the freezer to the microwave, he was shocked. He shouted, "No, Nonnie, no. I like my ice cream cold!"

Chapter 6

Styles of Conflict Management

Hippocrates (c. 460 BC- c. 370 BC), who is described as the father of modern medicine, identified four types of personalities. Around 200 AD, Galen (a Greek physician) developed a list of strengths and weaknesses to describe these four kinds of people. Galen attributed physical reaction to the "four fluids" of the body. These fluids were:

Sanguine. The sanguine (blood) person is warm, lively, and full of life. This person is extroverted, bouncy, and positively oriented.

Choleric. The choleric (water) person is hot-tempered, active, quick to react, and strong-willed. This person is not frightened by obstacles and is a workaholic.

Melancholic. The melancholic (black bile) person is perfectionist, who is analytical, self-sacrificing, gifted, and very sensitive. This person is usually very faithful and dependable and able to diagnose problems and find solutions.

Phlegmatic. The phlegmatic (yellow bile) person is calm, cool, collected, and easy going. This person is well balanced, with a low boiling point, not easily upset, very interested in enjoying people, and has a strong sense of humor.

In 1966, Tim LaHaye published *Spirit-Controlled Temperament*, the first modern book written in English for Christians on temperaments. LaHaye's book is resourceful in this area. LaHaye admits that the classification of the four temperaments is not perfect, but it is the oldest recognized classification of temperaments on record. The temperaments are another way to aid in understanding the differences in people.[1]

In the following Bible passage, LaHaye sees support for these four kinds of people.

> A generation curseth their father, and doth not bless their mother. A generation appears in their own eyes and yet is not washed from their filthiness. There is a generation, O how lofty is their eyes! In addition, their eyelids are lifted up. There is a generation, whose teeth are as swords, and their jaw teeth as knives, to devour the poor from off the earth, and the needy from among men. (Proverbs 30:11-14).

LaHaye associates a biblical character as representative of each of these temperaments. The sanguine is Peter; the choleric is Paul; the melancholy is Moses; the phlegmatic is Abraham. LaHaye has also developed a word association test by which a person can discover his or her own temperament. Studying this book is well worth the effort. I benefitted early in my Christian life from reading this book. The problem is that people usually do not use these Greek words in normal conversation and feel they cannot understand the meanings. Other writers have developed simpler methods, such as the DISC instrument, to determine temperament differences.[2]

DISC

The DISC is a personality instrument in which the letters "DISC" stand for the four temperaments of *(D)ominance, (I)nfluencing, (S)teadiness, and (C)ompliance*. William Marston, author and psychologist, developed this four-fold trait-based description of behavioral styles. Marston published this material in *The Emotions of Normal People* in 1928. Marston took Hippocrates' Greek titles and assigned one of the letters to each temperament. The work was further refined by John Greer and Dorothy Downey in the 1970s. Since DISC was never copyrighted, several versions and instruments appear under this name.[3] Two of the most widely used DISC instruments are *Uniquely You*, a publication by Mels Carbonell and *Understanding How Others Misunderstand You* by Ken Voges and Ron Braund.[4]

The strength of *Uniquely You* is that it combines a spiritual gifts inventory with the four DISC personality types. Churches seem to enjoy this approach.

Ken Voges and Ron Braund have likewise developed a DISC instrument. Their instrument is much shorter than Carbonell's, but it does not have the gift's inventory. Authors Gary Smalley and John Trent took the DISC and associated its temperament profiles with characteristics of animals.[5]

Table 3. Temperament and DISC Profile with Biblical Characters and Animal Characters[6]

Historic	DISC	Biblical Character	Animal
Choleric	(D)ominance	Paul	Lion
Sanguine	(I)nfluencing	Peter	Otter
Phlegmatic	(S)teadiness	Abraham	Golden Retriever
Melancholic	(C)ompliance	Moses	Beaver

DISC Overview

(D)ominance temperaments tend to take an active, assertive, direct approach to obtain results. A representative biblical character is Paul; the case study is Acts 9:3-19. The most appropriate way to respond to *D's* is to be direct, brief, and to the point. Confrontation may be necessary to gain their attention.

(I)nfluencing temperaments tend to be outgoing, friendly, impulsive, emotional, and reactive. A representative biblical character is Peter; the case study is John 21:1-22. The most appropriate way to respond to *I's* is to provide a friendly environment; never use confrontation if feedback is desired, and allow expression of their ideas.

(S)teadiness temperaments tend to prefer a deliberate, predictable environment. They like secure situations, and they value disciplined behavior. A representative biblical character is Abraham; the case study is Genesis 12-22. The most appropriate way to respond to *S's* is to provide a sincere, personal, and agreeable environment. Show a sincere interest in the person, and ask "how" questions to get an opinion.

(C)ompliance temperaments tend to prefer that things be conducted according to tested procedures and precise standards. A representative biblical character is Moses; the case study is Exodus 3-4. The most appropriate way to respond to *C's* is to be prepared in advance, provide straight pros and cons of ideas, support ideas with accurate data, and offer an exact job description with a precise explanation of how it fits into the big picture. Disagree with the facts, but not the person.[7]

The following chart shows the results of the survey from my dissertation.

The survey went to pastors in the East Texas area. The surveys consisted of a personality profile (DISC) and a conflict management style instrument. *Uniquely You* gives survey results for personality temperaments of lay members and those in the general population also using the DISC as the survey instrument. Findings reveal that the majority of all three groups surveyed are S's and C's, according to the DISC survey.

A Comparative Analysis of Selected Pastors' Personality Profiles and Their Conflict Management Styles[8]

1532 Pastors
 148 Pastorless Churches
1384 Possible Respondents
 763 Return 55.13%

Pastors	Church Members	General Population
D - 11.9%	S's and C's - 85-95%	D - 1%
I - 21.3%		I - 25%
S - 43.0%		S - 45%
C - 23.8%		C - 35%

DISC Responses to Conflict[9]

	Comfortable / Fear	
D—	Comfortable	Decisive
	Fear	Losing
I—	Comfortable	Enthusiastic
	Fear	Rejection
S—	Comfortable	Supportive
	Fear	Change
C—	Comfortable	Structured
	Fear	Being Wrong

Notice that each style has a comfort level in specific environments and the fear level indicates the person is in conflict and fears the possible outcome.

The DISC inventory is considered much easier to administer and evaluate than any of the previous personality inventories that I have used. Admittedly, there are weaknesses. At times, the instrument will fail to portray a person's correct temperament. As a whole, however, it is a valuable tool for ministry.

Styles of Conflict Management

Learning Activity

DISC Instrument

1. Complete the DISC instrument found on the next page.

2. Did anything surprise you about yourself?

Styles of Conflict Management

DISC Behavior Survey
(Natural Behavior)

> **Instructions:** Focus on your **instinctive behavior** and not what you perceive is the best response. Be aware, there are no right or wrong answers.
>
> **How to respond:** Rank each <u>horizontal row</u> of words on a scale of 4,3,2,1 with 4 being the word that *best* describes you and 1 being the *least* like you. Use each number in each line *only once*. Below is an example:
>
> [2] Dominant [1] Influencing [4] Steadiness [3] Compliant

☐ Forceful	☐ Lively	☐ Modest	☐ Tactful
☐ Aggressive	☐ Emotional	☐ Accommodating	☐ Consistent
☐ Direct	☐ Animated	☐ Agreeable	☐ Accurate
☐ Strong-willed	☐ People-oriented	☐ Gentle	☐ Perfectionist
☐ Daring	☐ Impulsive	☐ Kind	☐ Cautious
☐ Competitive	☐ Expressive	☐ Supportive	☐ Precise
☐ Risk taker	☐ Talkative	☐ Cooperative	☐ Factual
☐ Argumentative	☐ Fun-loving	☐ Patient	☐ Logical
☐ Bold	☐ Spontaneous	☐ Stable	☐ Organized
☐ Take Charge	☐ Optimistic	☐ Peaceful	☐ Conscientious
☐ Candid	☐ Cheerful	☐ Loyal	☐ Serious
☐ Independent	☐ Enthusiastic	☐ Good listener	☐ High standards
___ Total	___ Total	___ Total	___ Total
☐	☐	☐	☐

* **Note:** If your totals do not add up to 120, you did not complete the survey correctly or you made a mistake in adding up the totals. Recheck your work.

> This assessment survey is designed to determine your general DISC styles. For a more precise evaluation, the author recommends instruments using a "Most/Least" selection process which provides an expanded profile analysis.

Grandchild Story
(Pain or Pane)

I heard about this preacher who was supplying for a pastor who was away from his church. He took his grandson along with him. The pastor asked him to present the "children's sermon" as well as preach the main message. Because he wanted to explain to the boys and girls listening to his children's sermon what a supply preacher was, he called their attention to one of the windows in the church that was missing a pane and had a piece of cardboard covering the hole. The supply preacher said, "Boys and girls, I am here today like that piece of cardboard. I am taking the place of the pane."

After the service, his grandson said, "Paw Paw, you were not a piece of cardboard, you were a 'real pain' today."

Chapter 7

Generational Differences

In conflict management, an understanding of personality types such as that revealed by the DISC would benefit any consultant/mediator. Another valuable tool in understanding the way people react in conflict is generational differences. Understanding generational differences is important because people naturally divide along generational lines. Yet, the Bible says that Christians are to be one.

John 17:22, "and the glory which thou gavest me I have given them; that they may be one, even as we are one."

1 Timothy 4:12, "Let no man despise thy youth; but be thou an example of the believers, in word, in conversation, in charity, in spirit, in faith, in purity."

Generations respond differently to music, work, church loyalty, and conflict mediation. A serious conflict mediator must have some knowledge of these generational differences in order to facilitate reconciliation. I have developed the following chart on generational differences as a result of reading from several sources.[1]

See Generational Differences Chart that follows.

Generational Differences Chart

Generation Name	Born	World Influences	Work Characteristics	Church	Approach in Conflict
*Builders *Greatest Generation	Pre-1946	*Rural Life *Depression *World Wars	*Hard workers *Loyal *Saves for a rainy day	*Committed *Loyal to denomination *Prefer traditional music	"For the good of the church"
*Boomers *Me-Generation	1946-1964	*Television *Cold War *Nuclear Threat *Rock & Roll *Civil Rights *Space Age *Drugs	*Driven by values *When young, wanted to change the world *Now hold positions of authority *Work their way up the ladder *Women in the work-place	*Relationships *Wants to belong *Responds to Bible study & sermons	"The Bible teaches"
*Busters *Generation X	1965-1983	*Roe vs. Wade *High Tech *Video games *Berlin wall comes down *Latch-key kids *Divorce	*Eager to learn new skills *Want meaningful work *Prefer to work alone *Multicultural	*Small groups *House church *Contemporary svc. *Respond to worship music and mission trips	"Need to respect each other's views"
*Bridgers *Generation Z *Millennials	1984-2002	*Internet *MTV *You Tube *Terrorism and 9-11	*They don't expect to pay their dues *Opinions valued *Tech-savvy *Best educated *Value family, thus "Everybody gets trophy kids involved"	*Committed to the group *Desire interactivity *Interactive worship *Best around coffee table	"Need to listen to each other"

Learning Activity

1. Discuss the Generational Differences Chart in a diverse age group.

2. Referring to the chart above, share in what areas you agree and disagree.

3. Share from present or past experience how generational differences have contributed to conflict in the church.

Summary of Section 1

To be an effective conflict manager, mediator, and/or peacemaker you must:

1. Accept the fact conflict exists. To deny conflict is to delay reconciliation.
2. Work on not being so sensitive and learn how to overlook an offense.
3. Be honest and ask, "Is there sinful behavior in my life?"
4. Adhere to the truth that not all conflict is bad. How conflict is managed determines whether it is good or bad.
5. Learn to identify the signs of conflict.
6. Listen to parties in conflict and determine the level of conflict from their language.
7. Accept your personality style and identify the personality styles of others.
8. Ask if there are any generational issues.

Practical Applications

Prepare by reading and attending seminars on conflict management. Think through your own philosophy of conflict. Practice listening and observing others in order to identify their personality type and level of conflict involved. Experience is the best teacher. As you prepare and make yourself available, God will use you. Much of this material will make more sense as you engage in conflict management.

Section 2
Problems (Causes of Conflict)

Introduction

As related in Genesis, conflict has existed since the fall of Adam. When attempting to manage conflict, a person needs to be aware of the causes of conflict. These are the major problems conflicting our churches.

I became a Director of Missions in 1987 at the age of 37. I was the youngest Director of Missions in the state of Texas at that time. In my 21-year tenure as Director of Missions, I served in two areas and five different associations. My first area had 50 churches, with 20 of those churches in a single association. My last area had 115 churches and missions, with 50 churches in a single association. A Director of Missions wears many hats. He is a consultant to the churches, a mission strategist, a link to the denomination resources, a pastor to pastors, and an encourager. He also spends numerous hours with conflicted churches.

When I became a student of conflict management, I researched the causes of conflict in order to gain understanding. My research led me to a random survey of 220 Directors of Missions in Southern Baptist Associations in 40 state conventions. This non-scientific survey consisted of a one-page questionnaire. The research indicated that the major problems causing conflict in our churches are as follows.[1]

1984
Control issues
Factions
Leadership
Tenure
Interpersonal Relationships
Performance

1988
Communication
Immorality
Performance
Leadership
Control issues
Personality

1990
Personality
Performance
Control issues
Leadership style too strong
Attendance
Leadership style too weak

1997
Control issues
Pastor's poor people skills
Pastor's leadership style too strong
Church already in conflict
Conflict with staff
Church resistant to change
Pastor's administrative incompetence
Pastor's leadership too weak
Sexual misconduct
Worship style

Introduction

The survey of the Directors of Missions continued, but the instrument of survey changed; Directors were requested to provide only the top ten causes of conflict as they dealt with them in their association. The Southern Baptist Directors of Missions published the following list that indicates only the top ten causes of conflict.

2005
Control issues
Pastor's poor people skills
Church resistant to change
Pastor's leadership too strong
Church already conflicted
Decline in attendance
Leadership too weak
Pastor's administrative incompetence
Sexual misconduct
Conflict with other staff

Control issues
Pastor's poor people skills
Church resistant to change
Church already conflicted
Pastor's leadership style too strong
Pastor's leadership style too weak
Decline in attendance
Pastor's administrative incompetence
Sexual misconduct
Disagree over doctrine

2009
Control issues
Pastor's leadership style too weak
Pastor's leadership style too strong
Church is resistant to change
Church already conflicted
Sexual misconduct
Conflict with staff
Decline in attendance
Pastor's poor people skills
Pastor is at church too long

2012
Control issues
Pastor's poor people skills
Church is resistant to change
Pastor's leadership style too strong
Church already conflicted
Decline in attendance
Pastor's leadership style too weak
Pastor's administrative incompetence
Sexual misconduct
Disagreement over doctrine[2]

The top ten causes of conflict from my research and personal experience are: (In David Letterman style, the list goes backwards from least to greatest.)

10. Worship wars (underlying issue related to numerous conflicts listed above)
9. Church polity
8. Staff
7. Sexual misconduct
6. Incompetence
5. Church already in conflict
4. Communication
3. Church resistant to change
2. Pastor's leadership too strong or too weak
1. Control Issues

Conflict 10

Worship Wars

Story

The Administrative Assistant informed me that Mr. Stephens was here to see me. Though he did not have an appointment, I told the assistant to invite him in. Mr. Stephens, a man in his seventies, was a deacon at Danville Baptist Church and had been an active participant in the local Baptist association. Whatever was on his mind, I knew I needed to make time to listen.

Mr. Stephens sat down in the chair across from my desk and accepted the offer of a cup of coffee from my assistant. After some small talk on the weather, the Dallas Cowboys' recent loss, and the construction of the new dorm at our camp, Mr. Stephens revealed the purpose of his visit.

"Brother Smith," he began, "we got us a problem at Danville, and I need your help."

I replied, "Tell me about it, and you know I'll help you." I did not know the problem or what I could do about it, but as the Director of Missions I wanted to help any of those connected to the 120 churches in the area because they were hurting. Mr. Stephens shared his story as I sat listening.

"Well, Bro. Smith, it all started with our new song leader, Shawn Lawson. Now, he is a good singer, but young. The first thing he did was to start singing with that 'canned' music."

"Excuse me," I interrupted. "What is canned music?"

Mr. Stephens explained, "Oh you know, singing with those tapes instead of our pianist. It was like a slap in the face to Rose Mary. She has been playing the piano at our church for 40 years. For him not to use her talents is a shame. Bro. Smith, you know she is good. She played at several association meetings. Any church in our county would be thrilled to have Rose Mary as their pianist. Well, I heard Trinity Baptist Church can't find anyone to play for them. We are fortunate at Danville to have her."

As Mr. Stephens drank his coffee, I thought to myself, *What a shame.* Six months ago Danville Baptist Church was a church of 50 that had been in decline for 10 years. Then Bob Jackson, a young seminary student who was an excellent preacher, was called as the pastor. As he visited in the community, the church grew to over a hundred. When Bob first accepted the pastorate, the song service consisted of Rose Mary selecting the songs and Bob announcing the hymn number. No one could or would lead the music. Therefore, Bob called the hymn numbers, asked members to pray, made announcements, preached the sermon, and gave the invitation. After a month, he informed the deacons that he could not continue this routine and needed help. They all agreed.

The chair of the deacons said, "Bro. Bob, we agree with you. We need a young song leader to reach our young couples. If you can find one, we will make sure we have the money to pay him."

Bob found a high school senior, Shawn Lawson, in a nearby church. He was extremely talented for his years and had been in the All-State Choir and Band at his school. A leader among the youth at his church, he had publicly announced his call to the ministry. Therefore, when Bob approached him about being the Minister of Music at Danville Baptist Church, he was excited. This would be his first ministry position, and he would be making money to help pay for his college in the fall. He accepted the job, and for the first few months, the church was thrilled. The older members bragged around town about their dynamic young pastor and song leader. The church continued to grow.

Now I found myself listening to another story about a growing church entering conflict.

As he set down his cup of coffee, Mr. Stephens continued, "About two months ago, the young song leader came to the deacons meeting. We never let a song leader come before. However, the three new deacons said to let him speak. The song leader said his home church, Fellowship, the one that took Baptist out of their name. I don't like that. . ."

I nodded my head.

Mr. Stephens continued, "Fellowship wanted to give us their old 1975 edition *Baptist Hymnals*. Bro. Smith, since 1957 we have used that edition in the morning service and the yeller paper, *Heavenly Highways,* at the six o'clock service. Well, Bro. Smith, we couldn't see that using the new hymnals would hurt anything, so we agreed. But Bro. Smith, it didn't stop there. Young Shawn went on to say that he planned to install two projector screens and purchase a video projector. Grant, our oldest deacon, wanted to know why. The three young deacons fired back that the church needed the projectors because the young people like to sing off the screen. Well, after much discussion, we agreed.

When we got to church on Sunday, all the 1957 editions were gone and the 1975 editions were in the pew racks. The screens were up, and we sang two songs with hymnals and four without. No one seemed to mind until after the service. Then, Rose Mary asked to speak to the deacons and the pastor. Rose Mary started crying and I could hardly hear her, but she said, 'I have tried to be faithful for forty years, playing the piano, but if you men think I am not needed I will resign.'

Our chairman of deacons, young Roy Williams asked, 'Rose Mary, why would you think we want you to resign?'

She sobbed, 'Well, you replaced the hymnals that my granddad raised the money for, but you've replaced them with these new modern hymnals without asking me.'

Young Williams was trying to help so he said, 'Rose Mary, we certainly didn't do this to hurt you. These books were given to us.'

Well, Bro. Smith, the meeting broke up. That night when we returned to church, we found in every pew rack the 1957 edition hymnals, the 1975 edition hymnals, and the yeller *Heavenly Highways*. It looked like a bookstore. I never saw so many hymnals in one church. The two screens made the church look like a movie theater. We sang those 'little ditties.'"

I looked as if I didn't know what he meant by "little ditties."

He continued, "You know! Those little choruses, praise songs that my cousin Archie calls 7-11 songs. That means the song has seven words, and it's sung eleven times. Bro. Smith, I am afraid our church is going to split. What are we going to do?"

Story Results

After two months of continual conflict, the young music director resigned. The next month, the pastor resigned, and the church lost many of its members. Soon the church was back to below 50 in attendance and singing old hymns. A new group formed another church and sang choruses with a guitar.

Scripture

There is much diversity in the way churches incorporate music into their worship. Some have choirs in robes and sing traditional hymns and anthems while other churches have gone to praise teams in place of choirs. Some use hymnbooks, and some display the words to the hymns on a large screen. Some use only piano and organ music while others have a full orchestra or praise band.

The conflict is not over the right of an autonomous church to select its preferred style of music. The conflict generally comes when a new pastor or music minister seeks to change the style. If your church has ever had a conflict over music, you have plenty of company. These so-called worship wars have been extensively reported.

The heart of the matter in worship-wars is not the style of music, but the lack of understanding of biblical worship. However, there is something to be said for those who are sincere in their worship but still find certain styles of music to be troublesome.

Nearly all agree that music is a powerful force. God created music. Music is a large part of every church's ministry. The Bible instructs us to sing. Note the following:

> The verb *confess* appears in the Bible 21 times.
> The word *repent* appears it the Bible 38 times.
> The word *pray* appears in the Bible 117 times.
> The word *teach* appears in the Bible 118 times.
> The word *sing* appears in the Bible 145 times.

David Dykes, pastor of Green Acres Baptist Church in Tyler, Texas, preached a sermon on September 3, 2006, entitled "The Kind of Music God Loves."[1] He gave some advice on music based on Colossians 3:16: "Let the word of Christ dwell in you richly in all wisdom, teaching and admonishing one another in psalms, and hymns and spiritual songs singing with grace in your hearts to the Lord."

The Kind of Music God Loves

I. God loves different kinds of music. In Colossians 3:16, there are three different kinds of music that God approves.

A. Psalms

> A psalm is a song accompanied by a psaltery, a type of stringed instrument. When we sing a psalm, we are simply singing God's Word. The book of Psalms is a songbook consisting of 150 different psalms. There is a psalm for nearly every emotional need.

B. Hymns

Our English word for hymns is a transliteration of the Greek word *humnos*. Hymns may be defined as songs composed for worship and teaching. The obvious difference between a hymn and a psalm is that a psalm is inspired by God and is God's inerrant, infallible words. Hymns may be inspiring, but they are not inspired like the Scripture. Hymns are written by men and women who sat down with the intention of composing a song to honor God.

Dykes' comments on hymns reminded me of a time when I pastored an elderly man who lead music at vacation Bible school. He did something that irritated me, and I had to correct it. When he was leading the boys and girls to sing "The B-I-B-L-E," he asked the children to raise their Bibles. The he said, "If you don't have a Bible, raise a hymn book. It is inspired like the Bible." We had more than one discussion on this subject. I love hymns, and I believe the writers were inspired to write them. In fact, one of the more moving, special moments in my life was when Susan and I stood at the grave of Fanny Crosby in Bridgeport, Connecticut. Fanny Crosby was a blind writer who composed over 8,000 hymns. However, neither Crosby's hymns nor any other hymn is inspired like the Word of God.

C. Spiritual Songs

Spiritual songs are songs of praise. The phrase in the Bible is *ode pneumatikos*. We get our word *ode,* which means song, from the first word in the phrase. The second word *pneumatikos* means "the activity of the Spirit." The Greek word for spirit is *pneuma*, which means spirit, wind, breath, where we get our word *pneumatic*. An ode of the spirit is a simple, spontaneous song of praise, a song to the Lord. Today, we call these songs *praise choruses*.

The obvious difference between a spiritual song and a hymn is that the composer of a hymn sits down and works deliberately to structure a song. The composer of a praise chorus usually just starts singing, unpremeditated and unplanned. Some who do not like praise choruses will refer to these as "little ditties" or "7-11 songs," indicating that they seem to have seven words sung eleven times. Some say they are theologically weak and do not have the spiritual meat that hymns have. Those who like these praise songs enjoy the more contemporary music that accompanies them and feel they are involved in the activity of the Spirit.

II. Music is a Blessing

A. Music blesses God. "Praise the Lord, O my soul; and all my inmost being, praise his holy name," (Psalm 103:1). When we sing, we are singing to God. True worship is always an audience of one. We may not admit it, but we like it when people sing happy birthday to us. We like it because it makes us feel good that they care enough to sing to us. God is the same way. He likes it when we sing to Him. Psalms 22:3 says, "But thou art holy, O thou that inhabitest the praises of Israel."

B. Music blesses me. "Why are you downcast O my soul?" (Psalm 42:5). "Put your hope in God, for I will yet praise him, my Savior and my God" (Psalm 42:11). When I sing praises to God, I feel a change come over me. Jack Taylor, a popular preacher in the 1960s and 70s, used to say, "Praise is at once the most powerful tonic for a tired soul and the greatest therapy for a heavy spirit." Praise is the church's secret weapon against the enemy. Praise douses doubt and waters faith at the same time.[2]

C. Music blesses others. "I will extol the Lord at all times, his praise will always be on my lips. . .let the afflicted hear and rejoice," (Psalm 34:1-2).

I was on a mission trip in Africa with a busload of Americans when we encountered a large group of protesters. They threw rocks at our bus. Then, *en masse*, they approached the bus and started rocking it back and forth. Several passengers were frightened. All at once, someone started singing, then another and another until everyone on the bus was singing praises to God. Fear was exchanged for hope. The protesters backed away and allowed us to proceed. Music is a powerful force.

Music style need not be a source of worship wars. Much of the conflict surrounding music is caused by the approach leaders take to bring about the change. Some of the problem is created by attitude. I heard one elderly man say, "I personally do not like the praise songs, but if my grandson likes them and it keeps him in church, I can tolerate them."

Nationally known researcher George Barna, speaker at a Baylor University Symposium on Christian music said, "The 'worship-wars' have exaggerated the scope of the problem while ignoring the real issues regarding worship. The major challenge is not about how to use music to facilitate worship as much as it is to help people understand worship and have an intense passion to connect with God." Barna noted that relatively few churches have intense music battles; rather, most have too few people who truly engage God in worship. Barna said, "Music is just a tool meant to enable people to express themselves to God, yet we sometimes spend more time arguing over the tool than over the product and purpose of the two."

Barna encouraged church leaders to get back to basics. He states, "Many church people fight about music because they have yet to understand the purpose of music in the worship process. These battles are inappropriate distractions from meaningful ministry and fruitful discipleship. Christians need to be more zealous about and devoted to worshiping God."[3]

Suggestions

There have been many suggestions to resolve this conflict.

1. Pray about making a change in the worship service.
2. Communicate to the church before the change.
3. Listen and be sensitive to others.
4. Try a blended style with hymns *and* praise.
5. Educate the people with passages like Colossians 3:16 as well as about changes in other churches and our culture.
6. Try not to make a church be something it is not.
7. Consider having two different worship services: one traditional and one contemporary.
8. Remember the purpose of worship.

Learning Activity

Diversity Quiz

A friend of mine, Norris Smith (no relation), shared with me a Diversity Quiz that does not indicate conflict but does reveal the congregational diversity that can contribute to conflict. The purpose of the survey is to encourage a group to acknowledge diversity and to live in peace amid diversity.

Diversity Quiz[4]

Circle the number (1, 2, 3, 4 or 5) to represent your opinion. [One (1) closest to 1A and five (5) closest to 1B]

1A. The church needs new music to appeal to more people. |—1—2—3—4—5—| 1B. The church needs to keep its traditional music.

2A. Women should be ordained and allowed to pastor a church. |—1—2—3—4—5—| 2B. Women should not be ordained, and I do not want one as pastor.

3A. The church should be active in politics and speak against social evils. |—1—2—3—4—5—| 3B. The church has no business speaking out about politics and social matters.

4A. The church should spend a large part of its money on international missions. |—1—2—3—4—5—| 4B. The church should spend a large part of its budget on reaching people in their community.

5A. The church needs a larger Fellowship Hall. |—1—2—3—4—5—| 5B. The church needs to pay expenses for the youth ski trip.

Conflict 9

Church Polity

Story

Since he started pastoring at the age of 18, Richard (now in his mid-thirties) had pastored three previous churches. He had experienced conflict with the deacons in each church and either resigned or was fired from those churches. He had been at his present church, Calvary Baptist Church, for two years. Those two years were marked with peace and growth. Before Richard's arrival as pastor, the church had averaged 110 in attendance but had grown to 300, with several young families joining.

Richard regularly discipled and mentored five young men. One of their discipling sessions addressed the topic of church polity. Richard shared that he felt the biblical view of church polity was a plurality of elders to lead the church and that deacons were to be servants, not decision makers. The five young men accepted this viewpoint, and after a month asked Richard, "Why don't we have elders?"

Richard said that decision was up to the church, and he suggested they ask the deacons. One of the young men, a deacon, brought the subject up at the next deacons' meeting. The discussion became heated as one of the older deacons said, "Look, young man, elders are not Baptist. That's Presbyterian." Soon, the conversation of that meeting was the topic of discussion in several Sunday school classes, small groups, and fellowships. After about three months of this subject occupying much church discussion, the topic was brought to the business meeting.

Story Result

The atmosphere at the meeting was tense. Someone made the motion to elect five elders to be ruling leaders of the church with the pastor being the teaching elder and deacons to be servants. The vote was 98 in favor and 68 against. The pastor and the five young men perceived the vote as a victory. The next Sunday, instead of 300 in church, there were only 195 in attendance, and 100 of the members who usually attended weekly were not there and never returned.

Scripture

Polity is generally viewed as the way a local church organizes and governs itself. The scripture is clear that churches are to conduct themselves "properly and in an orderly manner" as stated in 1 Corinthians 14:40. Again, Paul commands orderliness from Christ's followers in Colossians 2:5 and rebukes a lack of discipline and structure in 1 Thessalonians 5:14 and 2 Thessalonians 3:6-7. Churches differ on how they are to be governed and organized. These differences date back to the beginning of the church.

In the New Testament, the words *presbyter* and *overseer* seem to refer to the same office or role. In Acts 20:17-35, Paul calls them both *elders* and *overseers*.

The writings of the early church (95-150 A.D.) attest to diversity among the churches concerning polity. Clement of Rome (95 A.D.) seems to make no distinction between bishops and elders. Ignatius of Antioch (107 A.D.) does see a difference in the two words and in the roles of bishops and elders. The Middle Ages saw the rise of Roman Catholicism, with the pope being the supreme authority in the Catholic Church. Luther and the Reformation rejected the single ruling of a pope. John Calvin, in 1564, argued that there is one level of ordained ministry and two kinds of elders in the church. Calvin maintained that those two types of elders are teaching elders and ruling elders. He based this belief on his understanding of 1 Timothy 5:17.[1]

In 1607, English Separatists, led by John Smyth and Thomas Helwys, migrated to Holland to escape religious persecution. After studying the scriptures, they came to the conclusion that baptism should be administered to believers only. Thus, the name of many churches is First Baptist Church. By baptizing believers without permission from a government official, they joined the ranks of the "Free churches." Based on scripture, the early Baptists accepted a polity that was congregational in nature. Today, there are as many different structures of polity and hybrid views as ever.

I. In broad terms, the three forms of church polity are:

A. Episcopal (Roman Catholics, Anglicans/Episcopalian, Methodist)
B. Presbyterian
C. Congregational (Baptists, Congregationalists)

II. In functional terms, the three major views are:

A. **Pastor-led church**: This view highlights the Priesthood of the believer and the autonomy of the local church. Proponents of this view use the pastor/teacher reference in Ephesians 4:11 as being the office directly related to the local church. This form of polity rests church authority with the local congregation. Scripture passages that support this view are Matthew 18:15-20, Acts 6:3, 13:203, 15:22, 1 Corinthians 5:2, and 2 Corinthians 2:6. Some points used to advocate this form of polity are that it is
   1. fair to the members.
   2. more conducive to developing loyalty and support of the congregation.
   3. likely to produce stronger, more mature Christians than other forms.

B. **Bishop-led church:** This form of polity is usually associated with the Episcopal and Anglican churches. This point of view offers a threefold order of ministry.

   1. The first order is the deacon. They are servants who are to aid the presbyter and bishops. Those who support this view cite Acts 6.
   2. The second order is the presbyter/elder (often translated "priest"). This refers to the leader/pastor of the local congregation.
   3. The third order is the *episkopos* or bishop, who is the overseer or superintendent. Those who stress this view trace their support back to the fact that there has been a continual office of bishop since 29 A.D.

C. **Plural-Elder-led church:** This form of polity uses a plurality of elders and has grown in popularity in recent years. The plurality of elders has actually become the source of additional conflict.

   1. Acts 14:21-23 speaks of appointing elders in every church and is used to confirm biblical evidence for this view. Titus 1:5 supports this also.

2. 1 Thessalonians 5:12-13 and Hebrews 13:7, 17, 24 support those who hold a distinction between the ruling elders and the teaching elders.
    a. They stress that the church is not a pure democracy and that the elders are not elected to simply carry out the congregations will.
    b. The elders are to rule and to oversee that the congregation is in agreement with the Word of God. [2]

Suggestions

I have no trouble with the right of a congregation to select their type of polity. However,

I do have a problem when a new pastor tries to force plurality of elders onto a church that has traditionally been pastor led.

1. A pastoral candidate should let the congregation know if he believes in plurality of elders before they call him as pastor.
2. Before calling a pastor, the church interviewing a pastoral candidate should let the candidate know that they are a traditional Baptist church and do not believe in the plurality of elders.
3. If church polity becomes a conflict, the church might be best served if the opinion of the majority rules.
4. Traditionally, Baptists have been congregationally governed, pastor-led, and deacon-served churches with Christ as the head of the church. I personally am comfortable with this model.

Learning Activity

Role-play

1. To help participants understand the various polity styles in churches, ask for three volunteers to act out each of the three major polity styles.
   Volunteer 1
       Role-play from the viewpoint of the Pastor-led church.
   Volunteer 2
       Role-play from the viewpoint of the Bishop-led church or hierarchy church.
   Volunteer 3
       Role-play from the viewpoint of the Plural elder-led church.

2. After the presentations, discuss the strengths and weaknesses of each style of polity.

Conflict 8

Staff

Story

When the Director of Missions of a local association of churches in Alaska asked me to mediate a conflict between a pastor and a staff member, I agreed. The pastor was fairly new to the church, having been there only two years. He was in his early forties and a graduate of a local seminary. He was the type of pastor who kept his office hours and times for visitation the same every day. On the other hand, the youth minister, who had served in this position for ten years, grew up in this church where his father had been a long-time deacon before surrendering to ministry. The youth minister attended a local college part-time and worked at the church part-time. He was not an organized person, and most of the youth activities were spontaneous. The church averaged over 800 in worship attendance. Though it was a large, growing church in many ways, it possessed a rural approach to ministry.

The Director of Missions and I met with both parties at the association office on Tuesday afternoon at 2 p.m. As mediator, I took the following steps.

1. I explained the mediation process.
2. I stressed to both parties that I was not a judge who was here to make a ruling of who was right and who was wrong.
3. I told them that I was present to help them come to an agreement.
4. I went over the mediation agreement and had them sign. (See the mediation agreement in Appendix A.)

5. I wrote on a whiteboard the word *solve* and used it as an acronym for the outline of our meeting.
    Share scripture and prayer.
    Open with statements and rules.
    Listen to each side of the story.
    Verify what has been said.
    Explore various solutions leading to an agreement.
6. I read some scripture and prayed.
7. I made opening statements, stressing the importance of listening and seeking a solution. I shared how this process works. We went over the rules they had already agreed to in the mediation agreement.
8. I listened to each side share his story after I stressed to each party the importance of not interrupting, even if he or she believed the one speaking was lying. I emphasized that they should allow God to deal with that, and they should concentrate on listening. I stressed that they should talk to one another and not to me. The room arrangement had been set up prior to the meeting to facilitate this.

Mediation Dialog

Pastor: John, I appreciate your love and zeal for the Lord. You definitely have a call of God. Clearly, you love the youth ministry. This church loves you. They watched you grow up. You are special to them. Your parents have been active, hard workers in the church for years. It has been a joy to see your dad called to the ministry and pastoring his first church. We will miss him as a deacon. John, I say all this sincerely. However, I have a few problems with you. I have tried to work through these. I've tried to change, and I've tried to overlook several incidents. This is why we are here today because when I talked with you on three previous occasions, I've seen no change. That is my frustration.

Mediator: Is that all you want to share?

Pastor: Yes, at this time

Mediator: Okay, John, it's your turn to share.

Youth Minister: I really do not know what the problem is here. I am doing my job like I have been for the last ten years. Bro. Steve, our previous pastor, had no problem with me. Bro. Bill comes here, and for two years I can do nothing right in his eyes. The deacons and the church seem to like what I am doing. I know our youth group is not growing, but we have the same number we've had for the past ten years. The attendance and membership have always gone up and down. That's all I have to say.

Mediator: Pastor, would you like to respond? Remember to talk to John and not to me.

Pastor: John, what I am about to say I've said to you before, so this should be no surprise. First, as the pastor, I believe I am your supervisor. I think I have the right to know what you are doing and give you some direction. Second, you have no job description, and every time I've asked you to develop one, you put me off. Thirdly, you spontaneously decide to take the youth to Six Flags and do not get any sponsors or permission slips, thus leaving the church open to lawsuits. Fourth, all the youth activities are fun and games. I see no discipleship or leadership training. Finally, the church pays you a good salary, but you spend way more time at college and working odd jobs. I know the church approved your college, but they still expected you to work thirty hours for the church each week. Frankly, I have not seen this. I want to make this work, but you have to make some changes. If you make these changes, this can work. That's all for now.

Mediator: John, do you want to respond?

Youth Minister: Why don't we get to the real truth here, Pastor? You want to be Youth Minister as well as Senior Pastor. You want to do all the teaching and use the lay people for activities. I will never be good enough for you. I am not going to answer your ridiculous demands.

9. As Mediator, I sensed the tension, and I moved to the next step.

Mediator: Okay, I think this is a good time to move on to the next step of our outline, which is the letter "V" that represents "verify." This is where I restate what I've heard each of you say, and if you do not agree, let me know. You can interrupt me so we can list accurately what you said.

Mediator: Pastor, I heard you say the problems you have with John are:

a. You do not feel he is submitting to your supervision.
b. You want him to write a job description.
c. You want more adult involvement in the youth activities.
d. You want more discipleship and leadership development.
e. You want John to have regular church hours.

Is that right or wrong pastor?

Pastor: That's fairly accurate.

Mediator: John, I heard you say the following are the things bothering you.

  a. You feel you have been doing a good job, and you feel most of the church members are pleased with your work.
  b. You feel the pastor wants you out so he can teach the youth.

Is that right?

Youth Minister: Yes. Those are the main issues I have.

10. *E* stands for explore solutions that lead to an agreement.

Mediator: We have listed seven items that have been problems we can agree on. The *E* stage explores possible solutions that lead to an agreement between you. Okay, John, let's take your second item first. You feel the pastor wants you out so he can teach the youth. Why do you feel that way?

Youth Minister: He is constantly telling me when he was a youth minister he had young men he was discipling and teaching leadership skills to and having Bible studies with. I would like to do those things too, but our kids are from low-income families and not like the rich kids he had at First Baptist.

Mediator: Pastor, do you want John to resign so you can teach the youth?

Pastor: No. I am not asking him to resign. I am asking him to recognize me as the pastor, write a job description, keep office hours and fulfill his obligations. I would like to teach from time to time. I did have a successful youth ministry in a large church at one time, but I am now the pastor of this church and want our youth to be discipled.

Mediator: For the sake of time, let's bring these issues to the surface and explore them more extensively. First, I understand, John, you grew up in this church. You did not have a youth minister as role model during those years. You are still in college. The activities you do with the youth seem to please everyone except the pastor. Second, Pastor, you are educated and trained and have experience as a youth minister. You see much more for the youth and want more for them. You see your role as pastor as an overseer, and you see yourself ultimately responsible for all the people of the church, despite the age group. John wishes you would just preach and leave him alone.

John, you have one view of the Youth Minister's job, and Pastor, you have another view. I would like for each of you to work on a couple of assignments, and we will meet back here in two weeks. I want to fill out the conflict settlement agreement, let you read it, and set a date to meet again.

11. Conflict Settlement Agreement (See in Appendix B)

Story Results

Both parties were supposed to meet again in two weeks. However, the youth minister resigned and is presently serving in the church where his father pastors. The church where the conflict occurred called another youth minister.

Scripture

Ephesians 4:11-12 states, "And he gave some, apostles; and some, prophets; and some, evangelists; and some, pastors and teachers; For the perfecting of the saints, for the work of the ministry, for the edifying of the body of Christ."

There is diversity among churches concerning the role of ministry staff. Some view all ministry staff as equals and expect them to work as a team with each minister having his own responsibilities. Some view the pastor as the leader with authority to supervise the rest of the staff. Some operate from a tradition of no organization while others operate from a business model with an organizational chart and detailed job descriptions. However, biblical evidence describes the pastor as the overseer. He is the one to set the vision and direction of the church.

Though churches may have diverse views about the role of pastor, most would agree with the foundational principles of pastoral leadership as described in 1 Peter 5:1-3. Pastoral leadership is essential to the life of any church. Without this leadership, a church cannot fulfill its mission. The New Testament is clear that God has designated the pastor as the leader in a local church. Acts 20, Hebrews 13:17, 1 Thessalonians 5:12-13, and 1 Corinthians 16:16-18 are clear that the church is to be subject to the pastor's leadership.

While the terms used may seem confusing, the words *pastor, elder, shepherd,* and *overseer* describe the roles of a pastor. All three usages can be seen in Acts 20:17, 28 and 1 Peter 5:12. Elder and overseer can be seen in Titus 1:5, 7, and overseer and shepherd are both described in 1 Peter 2:25.

A pastor's role as overseer is expressed broadly in two ways. The first role of the pastor is as director and leader. The second role of the pastor is to warn those in his care about spiritual danger such as sin, false teaching, and false teachers.[1] The ministry staff should support him, yet function within their own uniqueness and giftedness. The pastor should respect the gifts and calling of the staff members and disciple them, motivate them, and lead them to be successful in their role.

Suggestions

1. Before accepting a call to a church, a prospective pastor should
    a. be passionate about the vision God has given him in order to determine if the church will desire to work alongside him to fulfill that vision.
    b. spend time with staff members.
    c. make it clear up front that he wants the authority to hire or fire staff members. (If this request is not possible, he needs to weigh his call to this church.)
2. After accepting a call, the pastor should
    a. spend time with the staff, discipling and teaching them.
    b. be passionate about the vision God has given him for the church so that they will desire to work alongside him to fulfill that vision.
3. Before calling a staff minister, the pastor should
    a. spend time listening to his approach to ministry.
    b. ask multiple questions about his relationship with his former pastor, leadership style, and church.
    c. provide clearly written job descriptions, policies, and procedures as well as an organization chart.

Learning Activity

To help understand the difference between working against one another and working together toward a mutual end when resolving a dispute, ask two people to compete in an arm wrestling match. Give a piece of candy to the winner. Do this three times. Stop and say," You have been competing against each other. Now, find a way so each can win." Tell them there are only a few pieces of candy left. [2]

After the arm wrestling exercise, discuss the following questions.

1. What did it take for the two to move from competition mode to partnering mode?

2. Were there any surprises?

Sexual Immorality

Conflict 7

Sexual Immorality

Even though the media portrays Christians as prudes or Puritan fanatics, the Bible is very positive on sex. Proverbs 5:15-19 shows the joy of sex, as in verses 15-19,

> Drink waters out of thine own cistern, and running waters out of thine own well.
>
> Let thy fountains be dispersed abroad, and rivers of waters in the streets.
>
> Let them be only thine own, and not strangers' with thee.
>
> Let thy fountain be blessed: and rejoice with the wife of thy youth.
>
> Let her be as the loving hind and pleasant roe; let her breasts satisfy thee at all times; and be thou ravished always with her love.

The metaphor is that sex within the boundaries of marriage is a well of water that refreshes the soul and strengthens the body.

Unfortunately, regardless of the biblical instruction, conflicts caused by sexual immorality have increased in recent years. This chapter will present not one, but three conflict cases dealing with immorality.

Story

Conflict Case 1

As I drove into the church parking lot for the Pastor's prayer meeting, my cell phone rang. The voice was a familiar one.

His first and only words were, "Bro. Mike, can you come to the church immediately?"

I've been in the ministry long enough to know that when someone uses that tone of voice, I must take it seriously and give priority to that person's needs over whatever may be on my schedule for the day. I replied, "I'll be right over."

When I walked into the pastor's study, I thought I was looking at a dead man. His eyes were red and his face sallow. His wife was standing behind him as he slumped into his chair. He asked me to be seated. As he began to cry, I could not understand everything he said but was able to see it was serious. The pastor confessed to being caught in a pornographic sting by the police. The police had taken his computer and released him on bail. I listened to a bizarre story of how he was abused as a child, had developed an addiction to pornography on the computer, and had become flirtatious with homosexuality. His story was enough to make me sick to my stomach, yet it broke my heart for his wife, who was supporting her husband despite everything he had done. He asked me what he should do. I said, "We need to call your deacons together and share this information with them."

As we sat in silence waiting for the deacons to arrive, I thought, "This poor church!" The church had been growing and talking about relocating in order to build a new building. Now this. What a mess.

The deacons arrived and were surprised at the called meeting. The pastor sobbed as he retold his story. The deacons sat stunned.

The chair of the deacons turned to me and said, "What are we going to do?"

Story Results

Conflict Case 1

When I met with the church leadership, we all agreed the pastor was not to step back into the pulpit. They asked if I would handle the Sunday service. On Sunday morning, we read the pastor's resignation to the congregation. The leadership of the church and I had agreed that the pastor and his family could stay in the parsonage for three months and continue to receive his salary and benefits for three months. This was contingent upon his getting counseling. The church was torn over this news. Many wept in grief. Some wanted to run the pastor out of town and were angry at the leadership for giving him any assistance. Some felt the Christian thing to do was to forgive him and restore him to the ministry. He eventually moved his family out of state, and he is not in the ministry today. The church went through a yearlong interim, and the next pastor brought great healing to the church.

Conflict Case 2

Pastor John called me and invited me for lunch. I sensed he needed to talk in more than just a casual manner.

After we ate, he said, "I've got a problem and need your advice."

He went on to explain that their new youth minister was being charged with inappropriate behavior. This charge did not originate in Bro. John's church, but in the youth minister's previous church. The youth minister had begun a conversation with a girl on a social media website. They chatted each evening for about two hours. The youth minister thought the girl was in college and invited her out to eat. After dinner they went bowling, and afterwards he took her home. Over the next month they dated six times. On their last date, something happened. Her version was that the youth minister touched her inappropriately. His version is that he kissed her in a passionate way, but it was consensual. Summer ended, and the youth minister moved to a new church.

Pastor John got a phone call from the youth minister's previous pastor, who told him what the girl's parents were claiming. Pastor John met with the young man to explain the charges being made against him.

"All we did was kiss. It was passionate, but it was just a kiss," the youth minister replied.

Then Pastor John dropped the bomb. He asked, "Did you know she is only 14 years old?"

"No," he quickly said.

Turning to me, Pastor John asked, "What should we do as a church?"

Story Results

Conflict Case 2

This was a difficult situation because the youth minister's inappropriate behavior was at his previous church. In his present church, he was serving well, and, supposedly, everyone was pleased with him. When the leadership of the church learned of the allegation against him, they asked for the youth minister's resignation. As word leaked out, more and more parents felt uncomfortable with him around their daughters. He resigned and started selling cars.

Conflict Case 3

Nothing rivals the pain of death more than the pain of divorce. Pastor Cal entered my office, embraced me and literally collapsed, sobbing. I lifted him into a chair and let him cry.

After what seemed like an hour, but in reality was only a few seconds, he blurted out, "It's over. She's leaving me. She says there is not another man, but her phone shows numerous text messages to the same two numbers. When I confronted her, she said, 'They are only friends.' I've tried to get her to go to counseling, but her reply is that I should go because she doesn't need it. Then last Sunday, she stood up before the church and announced that she was tired of being a pastor's wife, sang a special before I preached, and walked across the street and joined the Methodist Church. She said she was never coming back. What should I do?"

Story Results

Conflict Case 3

The pastor's wife divorced him. The pastor resigned and went through the normal grieving process.

Scripture

We live in a sex-saturated culture. We have digressed a long way from the 1950s when television shows such as *I Love Lucy* had separate beds for the husband and the wife. When swimming, the public wore bathing suits that covered the body. Today, there is nudity on television, and bathing suits cover very little. In the 1950s, Hugh Hefner left his job at *Fortune* magazine to start *Playboy*. Today, pornography is a multibillion-dollar industry. Sexually explicit images are broadcast into our homes and across our computer screens. According to the *New York Times*, one out of four internet users access pornographic websites. The shocking statistic is that nearly 25% of these are women, showing that this is not just a man's addiction anymore.[1] *Leadership* magazine commissioned a poll of a thousand pastors. The pastors indicated that 12% of them had committed adultery while in the ministry.

Scripture addresses the area of sexual immorality.[2]

First, Proverbs 5:1-6 warns about the "adulteress," but the principles apply to all kinds of sexual temptations. The word *honey* represents words of seductive flattery just as do the expressions, "You're special," "You're attractive", and "I want you." Ultimately, what the temptations promise is always better than what they really deliver.

Second, Proverbs 5:7-14 tells how the father warns his son of the consequences of sexual immorality. Some of the consequences mentioned in these verses are that sexual sins drain energy, exact a financial cost, cause humiliation, and shorten life. For example, the average lifespan of a homosexual man today is 42 years. The Center for Disease Control and Prevention reported that "gonorrhea is the second most commonly reported STD in the U.S. It is caused by the Neisseria gonorrhoeae bacterium, and has been treated with antibiotics like penicillin since the 1940s. But over time, genetic mutations have increased the bacteria's resistance to penicillin, necessitating higher doses until the 1980s when several strains of gonorrhea resistant to penicillin and tetracycline antibiotics became widespread in the U.S."[3]

Third, Matthew 5:27-32 speaks on the topic of adultery. Recent studies indicate that 50% of married men and women will have at least one extramarital affair during their marriage. The word of God takes a very dim view of adultery. In the Old Testament, the punishment for adultery was death by stoning. Someone said that this may not have been a deterrent, but it sure cut down on repeat offenders. Concerning the seriousness of adultery, Jesus spoke about adultery being the only acceptable reason for divorce.

Fourth, Colossian 3:5 states that lust is a spiritual problem. Lust is defined as an intense and unrestrained sexual craving. Having a sexual desire is not lust. However, having an immoral desire about someone of the opposite sex is lusting. The cause of lust is the sinful flesh. Our culture makes a blatant attempt to arouse lustful sexuality. Every day, 2,800 girls get pregnant, and 1,100 have abortions. Every day, 4,200 people get a sexually transmitted disease. The best cure for all of these sexual misbehaviors is abstinence.[4]

**Baylor University
Clergy Sexual Misconduct Study**

In the average American congregation of 400 with 60% women, there are an average of 7 persons who have experienced CSM. CSM refers to a religious leader who makes a sexual advance or proposition to someone other than their spouse. [5]

Suggestions

1. Give careful attention to your devotional life.
2. Memorize scripture.
3. Establish accountability.

4. Do not start up the ladder of affection with anyone other than your spouse. Emotional adultery is dangerous.
5. Tell your spouse if someone makes inappropriate advances toward you.
6. Do not spend time alone with the opposite sex.
7. Keep the fires hot at home. Have a date night with your spouse weekly.
8. Get control of your thoughts. Long before an affair happens physically, it happens mentally.
9. Know this; you will get caught.
10. Confess, repent, and work on restoration when you fail.

Learning Activity

1. Divide into groups and discuss the sexual sins that have caused conflicts in churches.

2. Why do you think this area of conflict is growing?

Conflict 6

Incompetence

Story

The two couples were finishing their ice cream at the local ice cream shop. This was their routine after Sunday night worship. They ate quietly until one of the wives spoke up.

She said, "If no one else is going to speak, I will. What are we going to do about our pastor? Let's face it. He cannot preach. It is the same message over and over."

The other wife added, "He knows nothing about conducting a business meeting."

Next, one of the men voiced his opinion, "But he works hard on the building."

To this comment, his friend added, "Yes, he's a very hard worker, but he is incompetent as a pastor. Our Sunday school numbers are declining, the worship services are pitiful, and there is no sense of mission or direction."

One of the wives finished the discussion with, "You deacons need to have a talk with him."

The two deacons met with the pastor the following evening. One deacon started, "Pastor, you are a hard worker, but your messages are all the same. They are always on salvation and how we need to be visiting more."

The pastor responded, "Men, look at this building. Is it or is it not a beautiful structure?" The deacons agreed, and the pastor continued, "I work on this building ten to twelve hours a day, often all alone, without help from you. I have very little time for sermon preparation. The truth of the matter is a lot of our church members are lost and need to be saved. The Bible is a book about salvation."

One of the deacons interrupted, "Pastor, we have a lot of young couples who are struggling with finances and have marital problems."

The pastor fired back, "If they get saved and get right with God, they will be right with one another."

The other deacon jumped in on the conversation, "Pastor, many laugh at our business meetings. You don't use Robert's Rules of order. You get up in front of the people and say, 'God has revealed to me that we need to remodel the children's building.' You then proceed to say it will cost $50,000 and recommend we take $40,000 out of savings and receive a special offering Sunday for $10,000. You call for prayer, and the next day you're remodeling the children's building. We're accustomed to committees, reports, discussions, and then voting."

The pastor added sharply, "The way I conduct business meetings is the biblical way. I listen to God, pray, and go to work. Robert's Rules of order are the world's way. I am not aware anyone but you two who have trouble with the way I conduct business."

Story Results

Another month went by after their conversation. The deacons met with the pastor again and confronted him about his incompetence in administration. After an hour of intense exchange, the pastor said, "I quit. You people don't appreciate all of the work I've done on this new building. You are lazy and know nothing about being a Christian." He walked out.

Scripture

Incompetence is defined as ineptitude, lacking skill, useless, not qualified, inadequate, or unsuited. In the surveys in the Section 2 Introduction on causes of conflict, incompetence appears in the top ten. Most incompetent people are unaware of their incompetence. Dr. David Dunning of Cornell University reports that people who are incompetent are more confident of their abilities than competent people. Drueger, an associate of Dr. Dunning says, "Not only do incompetent people reach erroneous conclusions and make unfortunate choices, but their incompetence robs them of the ability to realize it." Incompetence is a sin that blinds us to our predicament. [1]

There are generally three ways ministers deal with their incompetence.

I. Some ministers try to cover their incompetence by overcompensating in other areas. The pastor in our story was not a good preacher. He overcompensated by working long hours on the building.

Those who try to cover their incompetence usually have an area they are very comfortable in and spend the majority of their time in that area, while neglecting other areas. A pastor friend of mine was excellent at visitation. He could carry on a conversation with anyone for hours. His day consisted of meeting with a group of men at Dairy Queen for breakfast from 6:00-8:00 a.m. Then he would check his mail, drop it off at the church, and visit with the secretary and staff from 8:00-10:00 a.m. From 10:00-11:30 a.m., he would visit with those in the local coffee shop. He always had a lunch commitment, which lasted until 1:00 p.m. He would drop by the church for an hour to answer any phone calls, and by 2:00 p.m. he went to the hospitals to visit with the sick until 4:00 p.m. He then went home to visit with his wife until around 6:00 p.m. From 6:00-9:00 p.m. he visited with people in the community. He ended his day with one more visit to the coffee shop and returned home at 10:00 p.m.

The people of the church and community loved this pastor. The trouble was that his staff stayed angry with him because he gave no direction or leadership. His sermons were hurried preparations on Saturday night. He did not like sermon preparation. He had never attended a Bible college or seminary. He did not like administrative work and covered it up by overcompensating in the area where he was most comfortable—visitation.

Luke 10:38-42 tells about Mary and Martha. Mary and Martha lived with their brother Lazarus in Bethany, a small village about two miles east of the temple in Jerusalem on the east slope of the Mount of Olives. Jesus was welcomed into their home by Martha. The text indicates Mary sat at the feet of Jesus to listen to Him. Martha went to the kitchen to fix a meal. Jesus was clear in verse 42 that of the two choices—serving or sitting at the feet of Jesus to worship—worship is the best. The text in Greek is clear. The adjective *good* could be used for the comparative *better* or even the superlative *best* (*New American Commentary*, p. 321). There is a comparison between the choices here, and Jesus is clear that nothing is better than what Mary chose. What feeds the soul is more important than what feeds the body. Jesus does not condemn service, but in verse 40 He calls it a distraction ("was cumbered" in KJV). Martha was fussing about the meal and the lack of help from Mary and missing time with the Master.

Often, ministers who are incompetent will become distracted from worship and overcompensate in areas like building or visiting. Worship and sermon preparation require sitting, being still, listening to God, and studying, all which are difficult for some ministers. It is much easier for some to go and serve.

II. Some ministers deny they are incompetent. This will often manifest itself by internal denial and external belittling of those who are competent.

The pastor in our story denied he was incompetent in conducting a business meeting. He declared his way was God's way and *Robert's Rules of Order* was the world's method.

Matthew 27:15-26 tells of the trial of Jesus before His crucifixion. He appears before Pilate. The stage is set. Jesus is arrested, charged, examined, and given the verdict of death. Pilate has the authority to issue a verdict. Pilate could exercise leadership and declare Jesus innocent. Instead, he leaves Jesus' fate in the hands of the mob. In verse 24, Pilate denies his incompetence as a leader by saying, "I wash my hands, I am innocent of the blood of this just person." Some ministers will pass off their own incompetence by placing blame on others. Be aware of ministers who consistently belittle or criticize others. This often is a sign of denial of their own incompetency.

III. Some ministers use their incompetence as an excuse. As Christian leaders, we can find all sorts of excuses for not obeying God's voice. Excuses are tools of the incompetent. Benjamin Franklin said, "He that is good at making excuses is seldom good for anything else." Gabriel Mevrier said, "He who excuses himself, accuses himself." Jeremiah 1:4-19 is an example of one who made excuses.[2]

Suggestions

All of us have areas of incompetence. What should we do?

1. Make sure of your call. God did not call everyone to preach.
2. Admit your areas of weakness.
3. Equip yourself to serve.
4. Grow in areas of your weakness.
5. Seek counsel and help.
6. Develop a small group in your church who will be honest with you and be accountable to them. They can, in a loving way, point out your weaknesses.
7. Listen to your wife. Competence can be learned.[3]

Incompetence

Learning Activity

How would you approach a pastor or staff member and discuss their incompetence?

1. List areas you have observed in which pastors who are incompetent.
2. Note the top three responses from each group and discuss them.

Grandchild Story
(Cooking up an excuse)

A family went to their grandmother's house for dinner. The meal was served, and little Ricky quickly started eating. His mother said, "Ricky, you know we pray before we eat at our house."

Ricky replied, "Yes, I know, but that's at our house. This is Grandma's house, and she knows how to cook."

Conflict 5

Church Conflicted/ Dysfunctional

Story

Canyon Rim Baptist Church started 60 years ago as a result of a split from Calvary Baptist Church. The split resulted from conflict over the King James Version of the Bible. The "King James only" people left Calvary Baptist to start Canyon Rim. In 60 years, Canyon Rim has had 24 pastors. In the last ten years, they have had six pastors. The church has never averaged more than 120 at any one time in its history. Presently, they are averaging 80 in worship.

A casual observation will confirm a pattern. A new pastor is called; everyone is excited. The church grows, and all appears to be well. Then, some issue arises; conflict sets in, and the pastor resigns or is forced terminated. Throughout the years, the issues have varied.

After being at Canyon Rim for only one year, one pastor tried to persuade the church to use Sunday school literature that was not Baptist. Some called the pastor a Pentecostal because of the music he liked. After a difficult deacons meeting, they asked the pastor to resign. He refused, so some withheld their tithes and offerings. This hurt the church. Some tried to get the pastor to resign because they knew he had no chance to survive. They cut off the water at the parsonage and refused to pay him. After a month, the pastor left.

Another conflict happened when a few of the young ladies got together and wanted to start an exercise class in the church gym. The pastor agreed and announced that the class was open to anyone who wanted to attend. Some of the elderly ladies thought the exercise class was disgusting. They visited the pastor and demanded he put a stop to the classes. This group claimed, "They don't have on enough clothes, and we have never had dancing in our church. These ladies need to be home caring for their husbands and children." The controversy erupted at the next business meeting. There were sharp exchanges on both sides. A vote was taken, and even though many did not vote, a decision to stop the class was made. As a result of this decision, several young couples left Canyon Rim, and the pastor resigned.

Another conflict occurred after the church called a new pastor. The new pastor and chairman of the deacons became best friends. They visited almost daily over coffee, and their families went out to eat together. As the church grew, the pastor spent less and less time with the chairman. He began to work with a small group of young men who wanted to go on a mission trip. The pastor asked the church to donate to the cost of the trip. They approved. However, word soon got back to the pastor that the chairman of the deacons was hurt and had commented that he was not sure if he was still needed at the church. His friends assured him that he was needed and that they would straighten out the pastor. Some met with the pastor and let him know he was spending too much time with the new people who did not support the church and he was neglecting the old members who did support the church. The pastor tried to reason with them, but they angrily left his office.

The pastor visited with the chairman of the deacons, but he sat in silence. His only response was, "I've been a member of this church for fifty years, and I've never been treated the way you treat me." To the surprise of many, the deacons called a business meeting. Very few of the young couples attended. One deacon called for the pastor to "vacate the pulpit." The vote was taken, and the pastor was given two weeks to move out of the parsonage. When the young couples learned of this, they were angry and asked the pastor to meet with them about starting a new church at a local motel.

Story Results

Canyon Rim Baptist Church continues to be a classic example of a dysfunctional church.

The pastor tenure averages about 15 months.

Scripture

James 4:1-12 gives some insight on conflicted or dysfunctional churches. A conflicted or dysfunctional church is a term used to describe a church that is not functioning in a healthy manner. Many people have been wounded and scarred by dysfunctional churches. The church is like the human body. The human body has systems, such as the respiratory, circulatory, and digestive systems that are essential to health and fitness. If any system fails to serve its purpose, the body becomes dysfunctional. Likewise, if any part of the church does not fulfill its purpose, the church becomes dysfunctional.

Causes and Cures for Conflict

1. Cause of Conflict—James 4:1-12
   a. James does not beat around the bush. He says that the cause of conflict is conflicting desires.
   b. Conflict erupts when these desires are selfish.
2. Cure for Conflict – James 4:5-12
   a. Scripture—James 4:5. James says to look within ourselves for the source of conflict and make sure that our desire is God's desire and not our selfish wants. We need to go to scripture to make sure what we want is not contrary to God's word.
   b. Submit—James 4:7. *Submit* is a military term, which means we are to come under the authority of another. We need to submit to God as the authority in our lives.
   c. Say *no* to the Devil—James 4:7. Evil is real, and the power of Satan is real. However, he can be resisted.
   d. Say *yes* to God—James 4:8. The Lord wants to walk with us. We need to draw nigh to God. God opposes the proud but gives grace to the humble.
   e. Stop judging others—James 4:11-12. If we set ourselves up as judge and jury, we are spiritually in trouble, and conflict is sure. James reminds us that God is the judge.[1]

Signs of a Dysfunctional Church

1. The church culture does not value the pastoral leadership. A church that has experienced a series of short-term pastors indicates the church's unwillingness to accept pastoral direction.
2. The leader is the only one who is allowed to think.
3. The church is controlled by a few of the members. When others are not allowed a role in leadership, they leave the church. The members in control think they are the only ones who are right.

4. The church is rigid and fixed in tradition. When a church will not allow new programs because of tradition, people will leave the church.
5. The church leaders have character problems, but no one will speak truth to them.
6. The church develops the "Hooterville Syndrome." This is where everyone knows everyone else's business, but the information is seldom accurate.[2]

In addition, a study of the sociology of churches will help a pastor acquire skills in recognizing the characteristics of various sizes of churches and what each size of church expects in its pastor. D. G. McCoury, author of several books on the sociology of churches, spoke at our association meeting in 1989 and helped me understand conflict in different sized churches. He has written several books on small churches that expound more in this area.

Sociology of Churches[3]

1. Patriarchal and matriarchal churches want a warm, fuzzy feeling out of their church and have the following characteristics:
   a. Church is family chapel.
   b. Pastor is viewed as a chaplain.
   c. Power rests on a key man and/or woman.
   d. Events are more important than programs.
   e. Church has high pastoral turnover, therefore, it is a difficult place for new pastors right out of seminary.

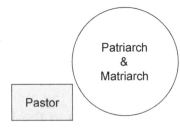

2. Pastoral churches have the following characteristics:
   a. Pastor is central.
   b. Pastor must delegate. . .or else.
   c. Church is the formula size for clergy burnout.
   d. Expectations are high and personal.
   e. Pastor contends with oppressive time demands.
   f. Pastor's popularity may determine church growth.
   g. Pastor's wife and children may experience difficult times.
3. Program churches have the following characteristics:
   a. Church has many leader cells and many programs.

b. Lay leadership is vital.
   c. Clergy is still central, but role shifts.
   d. Administration is responsible for recruiting, planning,
   e. training, evaluating, coordinating and such.
   f. Pastor has little time for "just stopping in for coffee in the kitchen."
   g. Pastor helps people arrive at a consensus.
   h. Pastor is also a motivator and trust builder.
   i. Changing from pastoral size to program size is difficult without crisis.

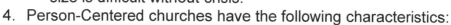

4. Person-Centered churches have the following characteristics:
   a. Worship quality is high priority.
   b. Music program is top notch.
   c. Sermon preparation and worship planning are top
   d. priority for head of staff.
   e. Senior pastor symbolizes unity and stability.
   f. Church has multiple staff and is collegial, yet diverse.
   g. Staff camaraderie is highly valued.
   h. Church's energy and momentum is generated by leader.
   i. Pastor is viewed as CEO.
   j. Pastor is pastor to the staff.

Suggestions

A friend of mine once said, "Jesus could not pastor 20% of the churches today." He meant these churches were habitually in conflict and so dysfunctional that no one could pastor them. This is why a prospective pastor should do the following:

1. Look at the history of a church. He should make sure God is leading him to that church. Dysfunctional churches can be turned around, but they need God's grace.
2. Be spiritually prepared when going to a dysfunctional church.
3. Quickly reach new people who will stand with him against the attacks of others.
4. Get the majority to speak up for righteousness.
5. Depend on the power of the Holy Spirit.

Learning Activity

1. From the list of the types of churches below, which do you think is the most difficult to pastor and why?

    Patriarchal/Matriarchal
    Pastoral
    Program
    Person-Centered

2. How do you think an association or convention should respond to a conflicted, dysfunctional church?

Communication

Conflict 4

Communication

Story

A concerned deacon called and asked if I could mediate a conflict between the pastor and the church secretary. My response was, "I'm always willing to help." He went on to explain the situation.

One afternoon while the pastor was out visiting hospitals, the water purifier salesman came by the church. He explained to the secretary that the annual lease agreement was up for renewal and asked if they would like to renew. The secretary, pleased with the water purifier, saw no reason not to renew the lease. She made out the check for the renewal and signed the lease agreement. She was authorized to write checks up to a fixed limit, and this fell within that limit. She thought no more about the situation and went on about her many other duties.

A couple of hours later, the pastor returned from visiting the sick, went into his office, and began answering the mail. The secretary stepped to his door and casually said, "By the way, the water purifier man, Hal, came by, and I renewed our lease agreement on the water purifier."

She turned to go back to her office when the pastor exploded in a loud voice, "You did what?"

The secretary repeated, "Our lease was up on the water purifier, and I renewed the lease for the same price for another year."

The pastor responded in a disgusted tone of voice, "I can't believe you did that. Don't you know I have been working to get the Properties Committee to agree to upgrade our water purifier to a reverse osmosis unit? Now you have made a mess. Why didn't you wait and ask me? I am the pastor."

The secretary tried to explain, "But, I did not know you were trying to get a better water purifier. You never said anything to me about it."

The pastor sharply responded, "I think you are assuming too much freedom in decision making. You need to operate within your job description." It was near the end of the day, so the secretary got her things and went home. When her husband arrived home, she was crying.

"What's wrong?" he asked.

She told her husband everything that had happened. He immediately called the chairman of the deacons and related the story to him. The chairman tried to defuse the situation and volunteered to talk to the pastor. He called the pastor, but the pastor was still upset and shared the incident from his viewpoint.

Story Results

The secretary was so hurt and upset she could not go back to work. As a result of this event, she and her husband left the church. This caused several other members to get upset with the pastor. The pastor contacted the water purifier salesman and explained the situation. The salesman agreed to work with them on an upgrade. Neither the secretary nor the pastor would agree to meet with the consultant for mediation. Both went their separate ways. The secretary, the pastor, and their families had been good friends and often spent time together going out to eat. Everyone thought they had a great working relationship. Sadly, a lack of communication regarding the water purifier incident caused a sharp separation between the two families.

． ． ． ． ． ．

Have you ever miscommunicated your thoughts? Miscommunication, or a lack of communication, can be very frustrating as illustrated in the next few light-hearted stories.

A man called his neighbor to help him move a couch. They pushed and pulled until they were exhausted, but the couch would not budge. The owner finally said, "Let's forget it. We will never get this out." His neighbor looked at him and said, "Out? I thought we were trying to move it in."

． ． ． ． ． ．

An American food company started selling baby food in Africa. They used the same packaging in Africa as they did in the United States. Each container displayed a picture of a cute baby on the label, but the baby food did not sell well in Africa. The company began to ask the people why they did not buy the baby food. They discovered that many people in Africa cannot read and thought the picture meant there were ground babies inside the jar.

・・・・・・

When Pepsi started marketing its products in China a few years ago, they translated their slogan, "Pepsi Brings You Back to Life." In Chinese, the slogan meant, "Pepsi Brings Your Ancestors Back from the Grave."

・・・・・・

A man went to visit a new neighbor. There was a dog on the porch. The visitor asked, "Does your dog bite?"

"No", replied the new neighbor. The man reached down to pat the dog and the dog bit him.

The man shouted, "I thought you said your dog did not bite!"

The neighbor answered, "That's not my dog."[1]

The above stories are humorous, but miscommunication or a lack of communication can cause serious problems. Here are some interesting facts about communication.[2]

> 7% of the impact of a speaker's message comes through words
>
> 38% of the message springs from speaker's tone of voice
>
> 55% of the message comes from speaker's nonverbal clues

If this is true and only 7% of the impact of communication comes from the words we use, then there is ample room for miscommunication. Poor communication is the source of most problems in both personal and professional relationships. Communication is essential to the health of any organization. Church conflicts over the smallest matters often result in the church losing its focus and purpose. Trivial differences can turn hostile and explosive, ending any chance for communication and reconciliation.

Scripture

1. Listen—James 1:19

In James 1:19 the phrase "quick to listen" means to pay attention when someone is speaking to you. People say they are listening, but are they? Good listening is a matter of concentration. People tend to be lazy listeners. They simply do not pay attention.

In effective communication there are six things that need to happen; all involve listening.

   a. Speak—a person says something to someone else.
   b. Listen—The one who is to receive the message has auditory waves enter his ears.
   c. Hear and respond—The listener translates the speaker's words into thoughts and feeds it to his brain.
   d. Feedback—The listener feeds back what he has heard. This could be verbal or nonverbal, like a nod of the head.
   e. Process the feedback—The speaker determines if the listener has understood the message. At this point the communication can go in two directions.
   f. Correct or continue—If the feedback tells the speaker the listener has gotten the message, the speaker will continue to communicate. If the feedback shows the speaker the message has not been received, the speaker must correct the feedback and start the cycle over again.

The key to good communication is to listen. You must concentrate on what is being said. The following are two examples of listening.

Example one: This communication is between a husband and wife.

Wife: "I am concerned about our finances."

Husband: Silence

Wife: "We need to talk about our finances."

Husband: "So you don't think I make enough money."

Rather than concentrating on what his wife said, he became defensive and missed the real message because he focused on his own feelings.

Example two: In this example from 2 Samuel 23, King David is an old man and is going out to fight the Philistines. He is camped in a cave. He thinks out loud, "Oh, that someone would give me a drink of the water from the well of Bethlehem, which *is* by the gate!" (v. 15 NKJV). Three of his men heard him and that night they risked their lives to sneak into Bethlehem and bring David some water. He was so moved by their devotion that he offered the water as an offering to the Lord.

David's men got the message because they were focused on the words of their beloved leader and not distracted by their own concerns.

2. **Speak**

We should be quick to listen but slow to speak. Some say God has given us two ears and one mouth for a purpose, meaning we should listen more than we talk. Some people are guilty of putting the mouth in motion before the brain is in gear. Be slow to speak. The spoken word cannot be unspoken. The Bible is full of warning about how the mouth gets us into trouble.

Proverbs 13:3 says, "He who guards his lips, mouth, and tongue keeps himself from calamity."

Proverbs 24:26 says, "An honest answer is like a kiss on the lips." The story of the proverbial elephant in the room describes people purposefully talking about everything except the obvious. Good communication causes us to speak about the issues, even the painful ones. When James cautions us to be slow to speak, he does not mean *do not speak*. He means speak carefully and thoughtfully.

3. **Avoid Angry Words**

In James, the Bible talks about being slow to anger. Anger and rage have destroyed more homes than tornadoes and termites combined. Explosive words hurt people and destroy relationships.

When Dwight D. Eisenhower was a child, he had a terrible temper. Once, when his father told him he could not go with his older brother, he flew into a rage. He began to beat the tree with his fist until his hands bled. His father grabbed him and took him inside. His mother began to quote Proverbs 16:32, "Better a man who controls his temper than one who takes a city." As he matured, Eisenhower asked God to help him control his temper. He later wrote if he had not learned to control his temper, he would never have been chosen as the supreme commander to lead the forces in World War II, and he never would have become President.[3]

Suggestions

1. Value communication.
2. Seek to improve your communication skills.
3. Practice listening.
4. Seek to understand before being understood.
5. Communicate clearly with a biblical attitude.

Learning Activity

Listening Self-Inventory[4]

Take the inventory individually, then discuss the results as a group.

1. Do you listen for the feelings behind facts when someone is speaking?

    a. Always   b. Most of the time   c. Not as much as I should

2. Do you generally talk more than you listen in an interchange with someone else?

    a. No   b. Sometimes   c. Yes

3. If you feel that it would take a lot of time to understand something, do you go out of your way to avoid listening?

    a. Often   b. Seldom   c. Never

4. Do emotions interfere with your listening?

    a. No   b. Sometimes   c. Yes

5. When someone is talking, do you work at making them think you are listening?

    a. Seldom   b. Often   c. Frequently

Conflict 3

Change

Change comes in many forms. The following three stories reveal how change in a church may cause conflict.

Stories

Case 1

Leadership Change

Pastor Dan announced his retirement. After 25 years, he finally succumbed to his wife's and his family's pressure to move closer to the grandchildren. The church had grown under his leadership. Most of the growth over the 25 years had come from new Christians. Thus, when discussions were held about calling a new pastor, most had no experience in this process.

Pastor Dan invited the denominational representative to visit with the deacons and church regarding practical advice for securing a new pastor. The denominational representative had some excellent suggestions. However, within a month of Bro. Dan's farewell reception, conflict started in several of the Sunday School classes where the lesson took a backseat to the discussion of what kind of pastor the church needed. The deacons tried to give guidance but soon discovered that several people in the church had little confidence in them. Many felt the deacons were Bro. Dan's hand-picked friends who were too old and out of touch with the majority of the church.

The deacons quickly secured the services of an interim pastor. This action shocked the majority of the church members who felt they had been denied their right to vote. At the next monthly business meeting, a lengthy and explosive discussion ensued. Most of the members left the meeting knowing that things did not look encouraging.

Story Results

The church selected members for a search committee and called a new young pastor within three months. The new pastor was totally opposite to Bro. Dan, who was a people person with visitation as his strength. The new pastor was more reserved. Within nine months, he was frustrated, and several in the church were calling for his resignation. Five months later, he resigned. By this time, several families had left the church.

Case 2

Organizational Change.

Hopewell Baptist Church was a traditional Baptist Church with a long heritage. The church was founded in 1856 and had been a model supporter of the denominational causes. Since its organization, the church had viewed the deacons as leaders. Every recommendation at a business meeting usually came from deacons. Pastor James resigned after ten years to go to a larger church. His pastorate had been viewed as successful with spurts of growth.

Dr. David Giles, who had recently graduated from the seminary, was called by the church in hopes that he could reach young couples. The church started growing as several young couples joined. Five deacons supported Pastor John and appreciated his efforts to reach the young couples. Some of their grandchildren had not been attending church and were now attending because of the pastor's efforts.

These five deacons were shocked when, at a business meeting, Dr. David announced to the church that all deacons were going to be given plaques and moved to Deacon Emeritus status. Three of the deacons did not understand, and all five of them sat in silence. The church voted to approve this action. The pastor then passed out the church organization chart showing a new structure. The chart had the pastor at the top and five teams to serve the church. He used TEAM as an acronym for his organizational plan.

T-Together in worship
E.-Evangelism and Education
A-Administration
M-Ministry

The church voted to approve the new plan, and the business meeting adjourned. The senior adult members were shocked and stayed late at the Dairy Queen, trying to understand what had happened. The deacons agreed to talk to the pastor.

Story Results

The deacons visited with the pastor for two hours. The pastor expressed his appreciation for the deacons' services but said it was time to change and let the younger men lead. One of the deacons said, "We'll see about this." At the next business meeting, the deacons got up and moved to return to the active role of deacons and do away with the TEAM approach. The vote was taken and failed. The five deacons and their families, as well as a hundred elderly members, left Hopewell Baptist Church. Thinking that their church had been stolen from them, they felt hurt, abused, and angry.

Case 3

Priority Change

For as long as anyone could remember, Sunday School was a priority at West Way Baptist Church. Several commented how the Sunday School classes had always had a larger attendance than the worship services. That began to change when the church called Mark Thompson as pastor.

Bro. Mark was dynamic preacher, and the congregation loved his mixture of humor and verse-by-verse preaching style. After a year of unusually rapid growth and overflow crowds, the church formed a building committee to plan the construction of a new auditorium. During the building process, Bro. Mark began to share with the staff how worship was going to change once they moved into the new auditorium. The new building would have two large projection screens, and there would be no choir loft, just one very large stage where a praise team would lead the music portion of the service. In addition, the worship service would be one and a half hours long and Sunday School would be reduced in length to 50 minutes. The pastor stated that the emphasis at West Way Baptist Church was going to change from Sunday School to a redesigned, dynamic Sunday worship service. Also, the church would have four major worship events each year in order to attract the community and the un-churched. Bro. Mark intended to preach messages on popular issues to help grow the church.

The staff, especially the Minister of Education, was shocked. He asked for a private meeting with the pastor, during which they had some sharp words. As the news about Bro. Mark's plans concerning the new worship service spread across the congregation, there was some discontent. The church, however, was doing so well that no one mounted a formidable resistance.

Story Results

West Way Baptist Church completed the new building and implemented all the changes Bro. Mark had mentioned. The church continued to grow. The Minister of Education resigned and went to a church he said valued Sunday School. A few older couples left the church because they preferred having a choir rather than a praise team singing "little ditties." The church continued to grow and Sunday School, while not the focus it once was, grew as well.

Scripture

Change seems to be the name of the game that organizations must play. Resistance to change is the nemesis that barks every step of the way. The problem is that people fear, resist, and try to sabotage the process of change. Change is difficult for some people to accept. Someone once said that the only person who really likes a change is a baby with a wet diaper.

If you were born before 1945, think of the changes you have experienced. You were born before television, penicillin, the polio vaccine, frozen foods, Xerox, plastic, contact lenses, credit cards, iPhones, and wireless internet. In your time, "closets" were for clothes and not for "coming out." A chip meant a piece of wood. Hardware was a type of store, and software was not even a word. Grass was something you mowed. Coke was a cold drink, and pot was something you cooked in. Wow! Things have certainly changed since 1945. Not all of the changes have been good. However, whether we like it or not, things change.[1] Change is a necessary part of life and essential for growth. Not to change is not to grow.

Reactions to Change

Commonly, when change comes, you will see these four different responses.

1. Some will be appalled—They don't want change because it will cost them something.
2. Some will be afraid—Their fear freezes them.
3. Some will be appreciative—Many people are ready and eager for change.
4. Some will be admiring—They are amazed, but they are not a part of the change.[2]

Mark 5:1-20 helps us understand how people react to change. In this text, Jesus miraculously brings about a physical and spiritual change in the demon possessed man of the Gadarenes. Notice how the above four responses to change are illustrated in these verses.

I. Appalled by change (verse 14).

When the demons were cast out of the demoniac and into a herd of swine, the swine herders' lives were changed. They were appalled and offended. Their income was taken away, and they could not care less about the man whom Jesus had healed. They cared only about themselves.

The problem many have with change is they have only themselves in mind. They have no love for others and certainly no desire to change. Paul reminds us in 1 Corinthians 13, "Love does not seek its own way." However, people who are hurt or angry sometimes become more and more self-seeking.

I am reminded of my pictures of the Sea of Galilee and the Dead Sea. The Sea of Galilee freely receives and gives out water that is carried away by the Jordan River to the Dead Sea. While the Sea of Galilee teems with life, the Dead Sea only takes water in and does not give any out. As a result, the Dead Sea has no living plants or fish in it. People who only take and never give are dead inside.

Some people today will not turn from sin, accept Christ as their Savior, and follow Him in baptism and church membership because of the change it may bring to their lives. We hear people say, "I don't want to give up my fun," "What will my friends think?" and "I may lose my job."

Are there things you do not want Jesus to change? What if He changed your job, your lifestyle, your income, your weekends, your traditions, or your family? How would you respond?

II. Afraid of change (verse 15)

When the swine-herders went into town and told the people how the demoniac had changed, they were afraid. The knowledge that someone among them was powerful enough to bring about such a dramatic change scared them. Just as in Bible times, many people today have metathesiophobia, fear of change. Some other "phobias" people have include:

Hydrophobia-Fear of water
Tonitrophobia-Fear of thunder
Entomophobia-Fear of insects
Zeusophobia-Fear of God
Nyctophobia-Fear of darkness
Zoophobia-Fear of animals
Ophidiophobia -Fear of snakes
Ecclesiophobia-Fear of church
Coulrophobia-Fear of clowns
Phobophobia-Fear of phobias

Acrophobia-Fear of heights
Peladophobia-Fear of baldness

President Franklin Delano Roosevelt said, "We have nothing to fear but fear itself." Fear is a very destructive force. Satan knows that and tries to strike fear into the hearts of men in order to make them ineffective. Fear is the opposite of faith. The Bible says that perfect love casts out fear and those with faith in Christ are not in bondage to the spirit of fear, but of love and a sound mind.

My wife listens to a CD of the *Chronicles of Narnia* every night. In this allegory written by C. S. Lewis, two sisters, Susan and Lucy, are ready to meet Aslan, the lion who represents Christ. Two talking animals, Mr. and Mrs. Beaver, try to prepare the girls to meet Aslan.

The two sisters keep asking, "Is it safe?"

The beavers answer, "Of course he isn't safe, but he is good. He is the King."

While we may fear change, we must face change. Who else but Christ can make the changes we need in our lives?

III. Appreciative of Change (verses 18-19)

The demonic man was appreciative of the change Christ brought into his life. Jesus had a mission for him to tell the whole nation what had happened to him. I wonder why the church is growing increasingly silent about the change that Jesus offers. All the statistics reveal that baptism numbers are down, church attendance is down, over 1,000 churches a year are closing their doors and going out of business, and fewer and fewer people are willing to serve.

Denominational leaders place the blame on the fact that we have not emphasized evangelism. Some place the blame on the lack of discipleship. Some say the problem with decline is because we are not starting new churches. Could it be that many are coming to church for comfort and not for change?

Arnold L. Cook in *Historical Drift*, states, "The inherent tendency of human organizations [is] to depart over time from their original beliefs, purposes and practices, which in the Christian context results in the loss of spiritual vitality."[3]

Joshua, after the death of Moses, led the children of Israel into the Promised Land. Joshua understood God's strong commitment to transmitting faith through successive generations. Immediately after crossing the Jordan River into the new land, he set up a monument of 12 stones so that all the people might remember the powerful hand of God and always fear the Lord (Joshua 4:20-24). The people served the Lord throughout the lifetime of Joshua. But Judges 2:7-10 records that after Joshua died another generation grew up, who knew neither the Lord nor what he had done for Israel. If we lose our appreciation for the change Christ has done in us, we will drift away from His ways.

Four Reasons a Church Resists Change

1. Congregational
   a. High value on traditional fellowship and maintenance
   b. Ongoing church conflict
   c. No vision
   d. Distrust
2. Personal
   a. Focus on themselves
   b. Lack understanding
3. Cultural
   a. View change as compromise with worldly culture.
   b. Idealize the past.
4. Fear/Faith[4]

Other Factors Why People Resist Change

1. Threatens power-holders
2. Threatens identity
3. Creates some sense of loss that produces grief
4. Requires learning new ways
5. Requires energy
6. Tends to show disrespect for past history
7. Removes people from their positions of significance and causes them to feel devalued
8. Exposes weakness and incompetency in some people
9. Creates subgroups who seek to sabotage the progress
10. Threatens the system of the church and dismantles its authority structures.[5]

Suggestions

When you are faced with change, do the following:

1. Remember your primary responsibility is to obey God's will. Jeremiah 29:11 says, "For I know the plans I have for you, declares the Lord, plans for welfare and not for evil, to give you a future and a hope." Colossians 1:9 states, "And so, from the day we heard, we have not ceased to pray for you, asking that you may be filled with the knowledge of his will in all spiritual wisdom and understanding." Paul prayed for the Colossians that they would be filled with the knowledge of God's will.
2. Remember God's priorities. We can accomplish much good, but we must stay focused on God's priorities of worship and evangelism. In Colossians 1:10, Paul prayed the church would increase in the knowledge of God. We do this by having time with God in worship and sharing Christ with others. Everyone, from time to time, needs to make a list of his or her values and clarify what is important.
3. Make changes needed to match your values to God's will.
4. Assess the church's attitude toward change. Read the history of the church. Talk to the older members to identify the "gate-keepers," the "bell cows," or the "E.F. Huttons" who are the members with influence.
5. Be honest when evaluating your own motivation for change. Ask yourself, "Am I trying to build my resume or build the church?"
6. Educate yourself on appropriate change principles. Read books, attend conferences, and visit with other pastors who have led successful as well as unsuccessful change.
7. Practice appropriate change principles. Relate all changes to the church's vision; earn the right to lead in change; involve others such as the lay leaders, and communicate continuously.

Learning Activity

Objective: To help the group understand the extent to which individuals will go in holding onto a position

1. Divide groups into pairs.
2. Give each pair a piece of rope that is 5 feet long.
3. Ask each group to play tug of war.

After 15 minutes or after one team wins, discuss the following:

1. How long were you willing to pull?
2. What precipitated your decision to let go?
3. How did your decision affect the other person?

Relate this to a conflict on change.[6]

Leadership

Conflict 2

Leadership Too Strong/Leadership Too Weak

While providing us with some understanding, surveys on causes of conflict do not tell the whole story. In every survey I have read, I have understood the cause of the conflict, but two areas of extremes have perplexed me. On the same survey, one group says that the pastoral leadership is too strong and another group says the pastoral leadership is too weak. A pastor may want to throw up his hands and say, "I can't win." Some people will never be satisfied. Some want a strong leader while others resist a strong leader. This section will examine both extremes in leadership. We will review two cases and hopefully have some biblical and practical suggestions.

Story

Case 1

The Leadership is Too Strong

After graduation from the seminary, Pastor Jason was excited about being called to his first full-time church. It was all he ever wanted—a parsonage near the church, a pastor's office, and a small town with plenty of un-churched people to visit. During the interview process, the Pastor Search

Leadership Too Strong/Leadership Too Weak

Committee had invited Jason and his wife to visit the church. They met in the basement that housed the fellowship hall and Sunday School rooms.

During the question and answer time, one of the deacons remarked, "You know, Pastor Jason, we are going to grow and will need a larger fellowship hall. We have been thinking about knocking out these Sunday School rooms and making a larger fellowship hall. Do you have any experience in building?"

Pastor Jason answered, "My dad was a carpenter, and I grew up helping him build and remodel houses, put up barns, and do just about anything you can think of in the construction business."

The deacon responded, "That's great!"

Pastor Jason and his wife moved into the parsonage on Saturday. He preached his first sermon on Sunday, attended the church-wide reception on Sunday night, and woke up early Monday morning ready to go to work. With his sledgehammer and carpentry tools in hand, he headed to the church basement and started knocking out walls to enlarge the fellowship hall. In about four hours, he had reduced most the walls to a big pile of rubble composed of sheetrock and lumber.

Three of the deacons stopped by to take Pastor Jason to coffee. They heard noise down in the basement and made their way down the long narrow stairway. They were shocked. Their eyes met with disbelief. One deacon finally opened his mouth to speak.

"Pastor, what are you doing?"

Pastor Jason responded, "I am enlarging the fellowship hall. You said the church had been thinking about doing this, so I decided this was a good time."

The deacons replied, "Pastor Jason, we have been talking about that for ten years, but we had no intention of doing it today. What about the new flooring, and where will the Sunday School classes meet? Oh no! We've got all kinds of problems now."

Bro. Jason said, "I'm not the kind of pastor to sit around. When there is something that needs to be done, I do it. There are three rooms upstairs we can use for Sunday School. I will go to the flooring company in town to order the new floors, and I'll install it. You look shocked, men. Don't worry. I will have this done by Sunday. Let's go get some coffee, and I will share some other plans I have with you."

Pastor Jason stayed at the church two more years. During that time, he remodeled the building, called the church's first full-time music/youth minister, and successfully reached several new families. He started small groups and led the church on a yearly mission trip to India. At one monthly deacons meeting, the chairman started what would become a two-hour session.

The chairman said, "Bro. Jason, you are a great pastor. You've done a lot for this church but, to be honest, you move too fast for most of us. Our elderly people are just tired from all you're demanding of them. Be honest. Most of what you started, we never voted on. You've bypassed the deacons and just started something without a motion, discussion, or vote. We've all talked and feel you would be better suited to a larger church with younger members. You are just too strong of a leader for us country folks."

Pastor Jason was completely shocked. He listened as the other deacons echoed what the chairman had stated. He went home that night hurt and amazed. The next morning, he called a friend to meet him for coffee. Jason opened the conversation by saying, "Last night I realized, after two years, that I want more for this church than they want." He recounted what took place in the deacons meeting. Before Pastor Jason left his friend, he gave him permission to share his resume with a larger church in a nearby town.

Story Results

In two months, Bro. Jason and his family were called to the larger church in the nearby town. This new, larger church had a full-time Minister of Music, Youth Minister, Education Director, and a Children's Minister. The church was growing, and Jason's strong leadership was what this church needed.

Case 2

The Leadership is Too Weak

John was a natural introvert, quiet and shy. He struggled with his call to preach. He knew he loved God and church, but meeting people and preaching caused him great anxiety. He shared with a pastor friend that every Sunday morning he awoke with stomach cramps and diarrhea because of the stress of getting in front of a crowd of people. John was a great one-on-one person with people he knew. He never missed a hospital visit, and he was great at comforting the bereaved. His office was always neat, and the financial reports, church bulletins, and newsletters were perfect works of art.

The church averaged 120 in attendance. As the town grew and subdivisions were built near the church, attendance grew to over 200. The church called a young, inexperienced man who attended the local university as director for the Youth/Music ministry. He was the very opposite of Pastor John. The youth minister was quick to think and act on issues, while John needed to contemplate issues for months before making a decision or taking action.

Things were going well until the youth minister lead the youth group in a fundraiser to help finance a trip to Splash World, the giant water park two hundred miles away. John did not know about the fundraiser because the youth minister always had an excuse for not attending staff meetings. John just let it go and assumed this was the way youth were today. After all, the youth attendance was growing. About two weeks after the youth traveled to Splash World, several parents asked to meet with Pastor John.

The parents took the opportunity to unload everything they thought was wrong with the youth minister. Their first concern was about his request at the fundraiser. He asked the girls to wear bikinis in order to attract more men who needed their trucks washed. Their next concern addressed the fact that on the trip to Splash World, the youth minister only had one other sponsor who was a woman of questionable morals and mental capacity. John listened and said he would speak to the youth minister.

John lost two nights' sleep worrying over how to approach the youth minister. He did not want to discourage him, but he knew the youth minister needed some guidance. Another week went by before John finally found time to confront him. The youth minister said the parents knew what was happening and were just complainers. He told Pastor John, "Don't worry. I'll handle this." John agreed to this arrangement and advised the youth minister to visit with the concerned parents.

On another occasion, some of the young couples who recently joined the church approached Pastor John one Sunday evening. "Pastor, can we talk to you?" one asked him. John nodded in approval and led them to his office. To John's surprise, when he got into his office, there were six couples waiting to talk with him. One couple was planning a wedding for their daughter and wanted to hold a dance in the church fellowship hall and serve champagne during the reception. John's stomach was in a knot. Since he felt pressured, he gave his permission against his better judgment. At the next deacons meeting, the deacons confronted him about this decision.

"Pastor, we have never had a dance in this church. We are Baptists," said the chairman.

Another deacon added, "Methodists and Catholics dance but *not* the Baptists. I can overlook the dance, but toasting with champagne is going too far. Pastor John, did you give them permission to do this?"

John was overwhelmed. He listened and tried to explain but was interrupted by one of the deacons every time he tried to speak.

Despite numerous difficulties, the church continued to grow. The younger members decided the church needed a gym or a family life center, so they approached the pastor, who encouraged them to pray. Six months later, one of the interested members asked the pastor if he was ready to approach the church about forming a building committee. John told them he was still praying. Three months later, after no decision had been made and no committee had been formed, several of the group asked for a private meeting with the deacons.

One of the young men spoke first. "Men, we love Bro. John as a pastor, but he is a weak leader. He avoids confrontation, and we have been waiting for nine months for him to form a committee to research and plan a Family Life Center."

This began the three-hour gripe session. The next day, two of the deacons who were John's best friends asked John to meet them for coffee. When they told John about the previous night's meeting, John told his friends that he had been praying about the matter but did not think it was a good time to approach the church. The two deacons told John they regretted having to tell him that many in the church thought he was too weak of a leader for this growing church.

The three talked a while longer and closed in prayer. John went home sick at heart and shared everything with his wife. They decided to take some time away to pray, so they headed to their favorite state park and camped for a week. Toward the end of their trip, John told his wife that he was not up to fighting this, and he did not want to hurt the church. "Mary, would you mind if I resign and go to work with my brother Jim as his assistant accountant? He has been after me to help him. I have my degree in accounting, and I know I would enjoy working with him." Mary agreed and promised she would support him in his decision.

Story Results

John offered an emotional resignation the next Sunday. The following Sunday, the church gave him a nice farewell reception, and soon afterwards, he and his family moved out of the parsonage. After a month as his brother's assistant accountant, he realized he no longer had stomach cramps or diarrhea on Sunday mornings.

Scripture

The Bible is clear that a pastor is to be the spiritual leader. New Testament passages such as 1 Timothy 3:1-7 and Titus 1:5-9 give the leader's qualifications. Acts. 2:17-35, 2 Timothy 4:1-5, 1 Peter 5:1-4 instruct the pastor on how he is to perform his pastoral duties.

By title and reference in the Bible, the pastor is the overseer of the church, setting both the vision and the direction of the church. Even so, he is to be a servant leader. Jesus was clear on this in Matthew 20:25-28. Servant leadership does not mean a pastor is to carry out every whim of the members; he is not a hireling or church errand boy. We must remember that a pastor is first a servant of God, not a servant of the sheep. He is accountable to God.

The Greek word *poimen* is translated *shepherd* or *pastor* and is a term of endearment. A pastor is to have a relationship with his people as a shepherd has with his sheep. The pastor is to feed and care for his people just as a shepherd feeds and cares for his sheep.

In John MacArthur's book, *Pastoral Ministry*, the chapter on "Leading" by Alex D. Montoya provides the following excellent practical requirements:

1. A good leader manages himself. Jesus accused the Jewish leaders of being unfit for leadership, calling them blind guides (Matthew 15:14, and 23:16, 24). A leader must live a controlled life. He must know how to manage his time, money, home life, and even his desires.
2. A good leader knows how to make good decisions. The proverbial saying "the buck stops here" applies to the pastor. Indecision or poor decisions will be costly in ministry.
3. A good leader communicates effectively. An effective pastor is more than a theologian. He must be an effective communicator. He must not only be able to preach but also be able to communicate vision and direction for the church.
4. A good leader is one who manages his leadership style. There are numerous leadership styles. Leaders of growing churches know that it is important to change style of leadership for the need.
5. A good leader gets along with people. Someone has said, "The ministry would be a great occupation if it weren't for the people."

    I used to laugh at that, but now I say, "Why are you in the ministry if you don't like people?" Ministry is a people business. A pastor may be a scholar, a great preacher, and an expert manager, but if he does not truly love people, he will never be a great leader.
6. A good leader is one who inspires. People have their ups and down and their ins and outs because of changing circumstances in their lives. A good leader must learn and be able to inspire others regardless of the situations people find themselves in at the time.
7. A good leader is one who is willing to pay the price. To be a pastor is not an easy task. It is not for the fainthearted, for the weak or for those looking for an easy life. Leaders must be willing to get into the war and pay the price.[1]

Suggestions

1. Manage resources and lead people. Have an understanding between managers and leaders.
2. Delegate responsibilities. Learn to use and value volunteers.
3. Resist self and honor God.

Learning Activity

Caution: Use wisdom and give no specific names in your discussion.

1. Give an example of a pastor you know whose leadership is too strong.
2. Give an example of a pastor you know who leadership is too weak.

Grandchild Story

The grandson was listening to Henry and Henrietta talk about their financial condition. Henrietta had inherited a large sum of money. She built a large new home and filled it with new furniture. She told Henry if it weren't for all her money, they would not have this big new home. Henry said, "Yes, dear."

Henrietta said, "Henry if it were not for all my money we wouldn't be sitting on this new furniture."

Henry replied, "Yes, dear."

Henrietta said, "Henry if it were not for my. . ."

Henry had heard enough and interrupted her. "Henrietta, if it weren't for all your money, I wouldn't be here."

Conflict 1

Control/Power

Story

Control/Power

Fairview Baptist Church, 110 years old, was located about 70 miles south of the Minneapolis-St. Paul Metroplex in a small town of 3,000. The Garrison family name was well known both in the community and in the history of the church. In addition to owning the local feed and grain store for over a hundred years, the Garrisons had helped establish the Fairview Baptist Church.

Sam Garrison had been the chairman of deacons the last 15 years. Billy (Sam's son) and John (Sam's younger brother) also served as deacons. Additionally, Sam's wife Sally was head of the women's organization and director of the children's choir. Sam's nephew, John Wyatt, led the music.

The Garrisons were not bad people. On the contrary, they were very giving people. They gave much of their time and finances to the church. Whenever finances got low or the church had a special project such as raising money for the youth to go to camp, the Garrisons always made up the monetary difference to meet the need. Some in the community referred to the church as the Garrison's church.

The church averaged about 170 in worship. Attendance would climb to around 200, then drop back down. The average tenure of a pastor at Fairview was three years, and the church had recently called a new pastor.

Control/Power

During the interview process with the Pastor Search Committee, prospective pastor Bill

Douglas asked the committee, "Do you want to grow and reach the lost of your community?"

Everyone on the committee said they believed that is what a church should do.

Bro. Douglas was excited about his call to Fairview Baptist Church as the pastor and came to the church with the desire to make evangelism the priority. This was not his first church. He had pastored a weekend church while he attended the seminary. Fairview would, however, be his first full-time pastorate, and he was eager to grow a church.

The first year, the church grew and averaged the highest attendance in its history. Some Sundays they would have 300 in worship. Some of the growth came from a new subdivision built outside of town. Some growth resulted when about 30 members joined the Fairview church because of a split in the First Baptist Church across town. However, everyone agreed that much of the growth was the fruit of Pastor Douglas' evangelistic efforts.

The Garrisons seemed pleased. Pastor Douglas maintained good relations with the family, especially Billy, Sam's son. Pastor Douglas and Billy were about the same age and loved to crappie fish.

The first sign of tension came when some of the "new members" volunteered to help Sam's wife, Sally, with the children's choir. Apparently, all went well until it was time for the annual Christmas program. Sally had done the same children's musical for Christmas ever since Billy was a boy in children's choir. This year, however, the new members wanted to do something different. At first Sally agreed, but the more she thought about it, the more she felt she was being pushed aside.

She commented to Sam one evening, "Sam, I'm starting to worry about our church. I miss the times when I knew everyone who was a member. There are so many people I don't know. In addition, some of those new people are trying to take over and push me aside. How do you feel about it?"

"Well, Sally," Sam began, "I understand how you feel. Pastor Douglas is a hard worker, but he rarely confides in me the way he used to do. Most of his time is spent with the younger men. I am also concerned about how much time Billy spends with him when Billy should be home with his family."

Sam decided to visit with Pastor Douglas and let him know how hurt Sally was over the way she had been treated by the new members. Sam said, "Pastor, Sally has given over 30 years to leading the children's choir. Would you not agree she knows what she is doing?"

Pastor Douglas responded that he was sure Sally knew exactly what she was doing. He went on to assure Sam she had done a good job for a long time. Before he could say more, he was interrupted.

Sam said, "Preacher, the Garrison family has given much to this church. We have seen preachers come and go, and we are not about to be pushed out by you."

Pastor Douglas was shocked, but as he tried to respond, Sam walked away.

Story Results

Things continued to unravel at the Fairview Baptist Church, and sides quickly formed based on those who supported the Garrison family and those who supported the pastor. Since many of the new members did not attend business meetings, they remained unaware of the efforts being made to remove Douglas as their pastor.

Pastor Douglas was unprepared when, three months after their confrontation, Sam stood up and said, "I move we declare the pulpit vacant." His brother, John gave a quick second. Pastor Douglas tried to speak, but several called for "question." A vote was taken, and the majority of those present voted Pastor Douglas out. The majority of the church was absent at the time of this meeting, but when they learned of the results of business meeting, they came *en masse* to show their support of Pastor Douglas.

After a week of shock and much talk, a group asked Bro. Douglas to start a new church in town. Thus, Grace Community Church was birthed. The attendance at Fairview Baptist Church declined from 300 back to 120 the next Sunday. The Garrison family was all smiles and was heard to say, "This is the way things used to be." However, Billy and his family moved their membership to Grace Community Church, which caused problems within the Garrison family.

Scripture

Control/Power or the misuse of control and power is destroying many of today's churches. According to the Director of Missions Survey cited earlier, the number one reason for conflict in the church is power struggles or control issues.[1]

The scriptures contain numerous examples of those who had power and these who abused it.

I. Biblical Truths about Power

A. Power originates from God. David declares in his prayer,

> "Thine, O Lord is the greatness, and the power, and the glory, and the victory, and the majesty: for all that is in the heaven and in the

earth is thine; thine is the kingdom, O Lord, and thou art exalted as head above all." 1 Chronicles 29:11

"Let every soul be subject unto the higher powers. For there is no power but of God: the powers that be are ordained of God." Romans 13:1

B. Power is given to whom God wills. Power is a matter of stewardship and is given for God's purposes.

"And he gave some, apostles; and some, prophets; and some, evangelists; and some, pastors and teachers; For the perfecting of the saints, for the work of the ministry, for the edifying of the body of Christ." Ephesians 4:11-12

"Let a man so account of us, as of the ministers of Christ, and stewards of the mysteries of God. Moreover it is required in stewards that a man be found faithful." 1 Corinthians 4:1-2

C. Power that is earthly and power that is spiritual create tension.

"For we know that the law is spiritual: but I am carnal, sold under sin. For that which I do I allow not: for what I would, that do I not; but what I hate, that do I. If then I do that which I would not, I consent unto the law that it is good." Romans 7:14-16

II Biblical example of power (Matthew 20:20-28)

A survey of the characters

A. Ambitious mother and sons (Matthew 20:20-21)

Salome, the sister of Mary, mother of Jesus (Matthew 27:56, Mark 15:40, and John 19:25), and her husband, Zebedee, had two sons named James and John. As Mary's sister, Salome was Jesus' aunt and her sons were his first cousins. They were right to think that Jesus was going to one day establish a literal kingdom in Jerusalem (2 Samuel 7:10-16, Isaiah 9:7 and 11:1-9, Jeremiah 23:3-8 & Ezekiel 37:24), but they were wrong in their selfish attempt to seek a high place of honor by using the influence of family connections. Their tactic was a common one, using the influence of family and friends to get ahead in life. As the world says, "It's who you know that counts."

Even though the sons of Zebedee appear to be humble by bowing down, clearly the request is self-seeking and bold. They were asking for the two highest places of honor, just like scribes and Pharisees who loved "the place of honor at banquets, and the chief seats in the synagogues," (Matthew 23:6). These two brothers longed for prestige and preeminence to be exalted over the other disciples.

B. **Answers from the Savior** (Matthew 20:23)

While Jesus did not rebuke James' and John's idea of the literal kingdom in Jerusalem, He did say they were ignorant for not knowing what they were asking. As He answered them directly, Jesus said, "You do not know what you are asking. For are you able to drink the cup that I am about to drink?" The cup Jesus spoke of was symbolic for suffering, which He had just described in verses 18 and 19. To "drink the cup" meant to drink the full measure, leaving nothing. The expression also implies endurance to the end, whatever the cost. This was Jesus' way of saying that the way to honor is not through positions of influence but through suffering in service. The one who has the greatest honor in the kingdom is the one who endures the greatest suffering on earth.

C. **Anger of the Disciples** (Matthew 20:24)

Though the angry response of the ten disciples seems righteous on the surface, clearly their anger is not one of righteousness. The other disciples were angry because they resented the two who asked for favor before they had the opportunity to ask. Furthermore, this is not the first time the disciples had engaged in a discussion concerning who would be the greatest. Mark 9:33-34 records that on the way from Caesarea Philippi to Capernaum they had discussed which of them was the greatest. Luke 22:24 records that on the eve of the Last Supper, a dispute broke out among them as to which one was the greatest. All the disciples shared the guilt of selfishness—wanting prominence, power, prestige, and control.

D. **Answers from the Savior** (Matthew 20:25-28)

Jesus uses the gentiles as an illustration. The phrase, "lord it over" (*katakuri euro*) carries the idea of ruling down on people. In that day, virtually every government used a form of dictatorship in

Control/Power

order to gain greatness through power and control. Peter warned Christian leaders against "lording it over" those allotted to their charge (1 Peter 5:3). The phrase "great men exercise authority over them" describes those who seek control by personal influence. Those who "lord it over" them in verse 25a use power and position. Verse 25b shows someone who seeks control by popularity and personality. They use flattery, charm, and attractiveness to manipulate others into serving their own selfish purposes.

The world's way promotes the principle of the pyramid—prestige and power of a great person built atop the many beneath him. In His teachings, Jesus turns the world's concept of greatness upside down. The world's ways of self-serving, self-promoting, and self-glorifying are the antithesis of spiritual greatness. Jesus says the world's way is not to be among you (v. 20:26). He impresses on His followers that the greatest is the one who serves; the one who wants to be first must be a slave. The word *servant* is *diakonos* from which we get our word, *deacon*, and *minister*. The word *slave* is *doulos*. A slave did not belong to himself but to his master. The surest mark of a true servant is the willingness to sacrifice for the sake of others in the name of Christ. The cost of true greatness is sacrificial service, and Jesus is our ultimate example.

Unfortunately, the church is often plagued with self-seeking leaders who capture the fascination of people who are willing to follow them.

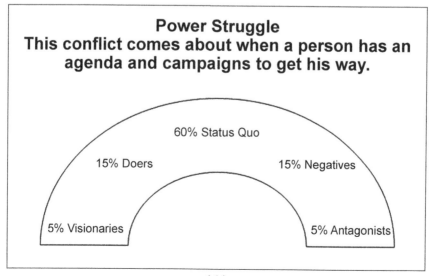

In every church, you will have visionaries, doers, status quo, negatives, and antagonists. Visionaries and doers have an agenda that usually promotes the church; the negatives whine and complain, but the antagonists' agenda seeks to destroy the pastor and/or the church.

> ## Antagonists
> (from Kenneth Haughk-*Antagonists in the Church*)
>
> **Moderate Antagonists** - These people seek to be involved in conflict or "What's going on."
>
> **Major Antagonists** - These people refuse to be reasoned with. Their demands cannot be satisfied. They are dishonest and have a drive for power.
>
> **Hard-core Antagonists** - They are psychotic. They continually cause conflict. They cannot be reasoned with.[2]

> ## The Clergy Killers
>
> 1. These people are destructive and toxic. They poison almost everything they touch.
> 2. These people are determined. They are not interested in a solution. Their goal is to destroy.
> 3. These people are deceitful. They work by spreading lies, innuendoes, gossip, rumors, and exaggerated tales.
> 4. These people are in denial. They cannot see their own problems. It is always someone else's fault.
> 5. These people are demonic. They are devilish. Cruelty, dishonesty, hatefulness, destructiveness, and dissension are their pattern.
>
> The percentage of pastors reported to have been run out of a church because of 5 or less people of the church is 23%.[3]

Suggestions

Possible solutions when faced with a Control/Power issue

1. Recognize the power brokers. A pastor in the process of interviewing and accepting a call to a church should identify the power brokers. Some power brokers are good people, but the pastor must build a relationship with them. The power brokers who are antagonists are difficult and can be destructive. A pastor who neglects and tries to bypass the power brokers will find himself in a difficult ministry. Some pastors are called to a church to break the hold of the power brokers and remind the congregation that the church belongs to God.
2. Recognize the power of relationship. It has been said that people do not care how much you know until they see how much you care. Generally, churches will follow a pastor if the pastor has worked and built good relationships. The smaller the church, the more critical it is to form and maintain good relationships with the power brokers.
3. Respond in a biblical manner. Do not fall into the trap of making all power brokers "the devil" and demonizing all who are against you. Follow Matthew 18, and go to communicate with those who differ with you.
    A. Communicate forgiveness. Seek forgiveness from those you offended. Give forgiveness to those who offended you. Preach forgiveness to your congregation.
    B. Create trust. Once trust and respect are broken or lost, it will take deliberate effort to restore. It also takes time.
    C. Consider resigning
        1. when you question your effectiveness as the pastor/leader in this church (an issue any minister will face at some point in his ministry)
        2. when staying is a risk to your physical, emotional or spiritual health.
        3. when a majority is against you.
        4. when you have committed a biblical offense such as moral failure or doctrinal violation.
        5. when your wife or confident friends pray with you and ask you to consider resigning.
        6. when God opens up another ministry or clearly reveals resigning is what you should do.
    D. Consider confronting the power brokers. Often, a pastor resigns and leaves prematurely. This can often be against God's will.
        1. Confront the power broker in a biblical manner as Matthew 18 outlines.

2. Consider that God has you in this position to redirect the church back to its mission and purpose. Mordecai's words to Queen Esther is Esther 4:14,

> "For if thou altogether holdest thy peace at this time, then shall there enlargement and deliverance arise to the Jews from another place; but thou and thy father's house shall be destroyed: and who knoweth whether thou art come to the kingdom for such a time as this?"

E. In conflict, ask if the issue is biblical
F. Respond in a biblical manner.
G. Understand control issues.
   1. Satan uses power and control issues as a temptation to cause the church to lose focus.
   2. God is to rule the church, not man.
   3. Influential members of the church have authority and trust because they have earned it. Pastors need to earn trust.
   4. In a typical church, the pastor is granted the privilege of temporary leadership because of his position. After the honeymoon stage, it will take time to earn long-term leadership.
   5. Decisions within the church are best made through prayerful considerations as the church seeks God's leadership and not through dependence on mankind's wisdom, preferences, or opinions.
H. Neutralize Power and Control Issues
   1. Be a servant leader.
   2. Learn to share the ministry with volunteer leaders in the church.
   3. Focus on what God can do through the church and not on building your own reputation or resume.
   4. Accept the fact that some people will always resist your attempts at leadership and that you will have to deal with them in love.
   5. Pray for God's guidance and power.

Learning Activity

1. Divide into small groups and share how you have dealt with power brokers.
2. Reassemble into one large group, and list on the board ways to deal with power brokers.

Summary of Section 2

Reading Section 2 may have made some readers heart sick. Anyone who has been through a church conflict is familiar with the terrible upheaval of emotions when Christians are pitted against one another. It is disgusting to see once highly respected church members participate in slander, anger, bitterness, gossip, rebellion, and pride. Some will try to excuse anger as "standing on principle" while others will disguise slander and gossip as a "search for the truth."

Conflict not only hurts individuals but also divides families, splits church congregations, and impacts missions, ministries, and support to a denomination. Most importantly, the gospel witness to a lost community suffers as well.

Conflict is often a war in which only the devil wins. Jesus warns us in Matthew 12:25 that when our house is divided, it "shall not stand."[1]

The first conflict occurred in Heaven. Satan was known as Lucifer or *Hillel Ben Shahar* in the Hebrew language. The name Hillel came from the root word, *Hallel*, which means to praise, worship, or adore. Ben Shahar means, "Son of the dawn." Lucifer was the chief worship leader in Heaven. He had gifts of leadership and creativity in music. Fueled by jealousy and ambition, he led a third of the angels to rebel against God (Isaiah 14:12-14, Revelation 12, Matthew 25:41). Satan means "one who opposes" or "adversary." Satan will oppose any healing and reconciliation in a conflict. The word *devil* means "slander." To slander means more than "to speak evil of one another." Literally, it means, "one who puts himself or something between two in order to divide them." Ever since his rebellion in Heaven, Satan's goal has been to divide—to divide friendships, marriages, churches, and nations.[2]

Summary of Section 2

In a conflict there are usually four groups.

Group One

Group one is made up of people who initiate conflict because they have unresolved personal issues. Often, these people will manifest their internal strife outwardly toward the pastor, staff, or in the church's direction. They want change in the church. They are unhappy people.

Group Two

Group two is usually made up of supporters of the current pastor, staff, and direction of the church. They are faithful in giving and attendance.

Group Three

Group three are those who are caught in the middle and have friends on both sides of the issues. They hear slander and gossip from both directions. They sometimes are not "in the know" and are very confused as to why the conflict exists. Often, this group will just drop out and stop attending church.

Group Four

Group four consists of the family members of the church leaders. These are innocent spouses and children who are hurt by the fact that one of their loved ones is in conflict. They hear all the talk and feel all the attacks, yet they are helpless to do anything. After a conflict, wives may plead with their husbands to seek another career, and some wives may experience health deterioration. Conflict may even put a hardship on the marriage. Often the memory of a church conflict incubates long in children, and many walk away from the church or their denomination when they leave home.

The judgment Jesus pronounced in Matthew 18:6 may well apply to these innocent family members. "But whoso shall offend one of these little ones which believe in me, it were better for him that a millstone were hanged about his neck, and that he were drowned in the depth of the sea."

A serious student of church conflict must gain an understanding of the causes of conflict but must never forget Paul's words in Ephesians 6:12, "For we wrestle not against flesh and blood, but against principalities, against powers, against the rulers of the darkness of this world, against spiritual wickedness in high places."

Section 3
Possibilities (Cures for Conflict)

Introduction

A person who only views conflict in the negative will miss seeing what God can do. Every conflict presents multiple possibilities. This last section will present three reactions or practical suggestions for response to conflict.

1. **Education**. Education takes a proactive approach. The more informed people are, the less apprehensive they are. Education is part of the disciple-making responsibility of the church. Church leaders need to educate their members about how to relate to God and how to relate to one another. In Matthew 22:37-40, Jesus said,

   "Thou shalt love the Lord thy God with all thy heart, and with all thy soul, and with all thy mind. This is the first and great commandment. And the second is like unto it, Thou shalt love thy neighbor as thyself. On these two commandments hang all the law and the prophets."

2. **Mediation**. Mediation, a possible solution to conflict, is a part of the Matthew 18 principle. Mediation requires a skilled, experienced mediator who can give hope to difficult situations. Paul reminds us in 2 Corinthians 5:18,

   "And all things are of God, who hath reconciled us to himself by Jesus Christ, and hath given to us the ministry of reconciliation;"

3. **Restoration**. While conflict hurts ministers and members of churches, restoration is a healing process. The church often neglects these wounded believers and many become a statistic in the inactive church list. Much more can be done in the area of restoration in order to reclaim and restore these saints. Galatians 6:1 applies to many situations.[1]

   "Brethren, if a man be overtaken in a fault, ye which are spiritual, restore such an one in the spirit of meekness; considering thyself, lest thou also be tempted."

   Hosea 6:1 says, "Come, and let us return unto the Lord: for he hath torn, and he will heal us; he hath smitten, and he will bind us up."

Grandchild Story
(Shades of Red)

Not understanding that some statements are best unrepeated, grandchildren can embarrass you at times by saying what they have heard others say. Such was the case between a grandfather and his grandson. After a worship service, the little boy handed the preacher a dollar bill. The preacher asked, "Why didn't you put the dollar in the offering plate when it was passed?"

The little boy replied, "I wanted to make sure you got it because my granddad said you were the poorest preacher he ever heard."

Chapter 1

Education

Church leaders have a responsibility to equip their people through education. This equipping process should not only have an example of how to share the gospel but also include an example of how to respond to and manage conflict in a biblical way.

I. Biblical ways to respond to conflict

   A. **Attitude:** Someone said, "A bad attitude is like a flat tire. You can't go anywhere until you change it." God's people need to be educated concerning how to maintain a proper attitude toward conflict. The ABCs of a proper attitude toward conflict are:
   1. **Admit** conflicts exist.
    Some want to approach conflict like the proverbial ostrich with its head in the sand. This attitude is not good and may delay the inevitable. The Bible contains at least 133 conflict examples. Obviously, the Bible admits conflict exists and so should we.
   2. **Believe** conflict can be healthy and is not always unhealthy.
   3. **Communicate**—Matthew 18:15-17 says to deal with conflict as follows:

   > "Moreover if thy brother shall trespass against thee, go and tell him his fault between thee and him alone: if he shall hear thee, thou hast gained thy brother. But if he will not hear thee, then take with thee one or two more, that

Education

in the mouth of two or three witnesses every word may be established. And if he shall neglect to hear them, tell it unto the church: but if he neglects to hear the church, let him be unto thee as an heathen man and a publican."

Conflict is best resolved when the fewest possible people are involved. Matthew 18:15-17 demonstrates Jesus' conflict management plan, and it is summarized below.[1]
  a. **Go privately** and confront—Take the initiative, whether you have wronged someone or they have wronged you. Do not gossip. Go privately to the individual.
  b. **Go promptly**. The longer you wait, the more time Satan has to cause confusion.
  c. **Go prayerfully**. James 1:5 says,

  > "If any of you lack wisdom, let him ask of God, that giveth to all men liberally, and upbraideth not; and it shall be given him."

  Conflict is a spiritual battle that must be approached after much wisdom-seeking prayer.
  d. **Go persistently**. If the conflict cannot be resolved in private, take someone with you or seek the service of a mediator. Matthew 18:16 says,

  > "But if they will not listen, take one or two others along, so that every matter may be established by the testimony of two or three witnesses."

  e. **Go purposefully** (church discipline). If the conflict cannot be resolved otherwise, Jesus instructs, "Tell it to the church," Matthew 18:17 (NIV). This is to be done in a way that is consistent with the intent of Matthew 18. The purpose of church discipline is to lead to repentance and restoration. [2]

B. <u>**Actions to take in conflict**</u>
  1. <u>**What to do when you are offended**</u>
     a. Take the initiative. Matthew 18:15
     b. Ask yourself, "Did I do anything to contribute to this wrong?"
     c. Learn to overlook and not be so easily offended.[3]
     d. Pray before you confront.

e. Confront privately with humility. "Have I done something that has caused you to be angry with me?" "Can you help me understand why you said. . .?"
f. Listen. "Seek to understand their view before being understood." Dr. John Drakeford, a professor of mine in seminary states in his book entitled *The Awesome Power of the Listening Ear* that high emotions during conflict can be lowered by the power of listening attentively to the other side's point of view.[4]
g. Forgive. The Greek word *aphiemi* translated is "forgive," which means to let go, release, or cancel a debt. Forgiveness is not a feeling but rather a decision and an action of the will.[5]

2. **What to do when you are the offender**
   a. Get right with God. Psalm 41:1-4
   b. Confess to God. John 1:9
   c. Repent. 2 Corinthians 7:9-10
   d. Address everyone you offended.
   e. Apologize. "I'm sorry. Will you forgive me?"
   f. Make restitution toward those you hurt. Lies need to be confessed, but gossip and slander must be repudiated.
   g. Alter your behavior and accept God's forgiveness.[6]

3. **What to do when you observe an offense**
   a. Follow Galatians 6:1 and James 5: 19-20.

      "Brethren, if a man be overtaken in a fault, ye which are spiritual, restore such an one in the spirit of meekness; considering thyself, lest thou also be tempted."

      James 5:19-20 states, "Brethren, if any of you do err from the truth, and one convert him; Let him know, that he which converteth the sinner from the error of his way shall save a soul from death, and shall hide a multitude of sins."

   b. Examine your own spiritual condition.
   c. Pray.
   d. Ask yourself these questions before confronting someone.
      1) Is the issue dishonoring God? Romans 1:23-24
      2) Is the issue damaging a relationship? 2 Timothy 4:2-4 and Matthew 18:14.
      3) Is the issue hurting the one offended? Proverbs 24:11-12
   e. Meet face-to-face in the spirit of gentleness by using such statements as "I admit I'm a long way from being perfect, and I'm not here to condemn you, but I care. . ."

f. Confront the specific sin issue. Speak truth in love, Ephesians 4:15. Be willing to forgive and reconcile, Ephesians 4:32.
4. **Conflict Management Team**
   a. Lead your church to adopt a conflict management process.
   b. Elect a conflict management team or a group of peacemakers. Since Acts 6 seems to indicate the first need of deacons in the church was to resolve a conflict, this team could consist of deacons
   c. Train this qualified team.
   d. Adopt a church process and encourage the members to follow this process.
5. **Reasons for church discipline**
   a. Flagrant and arrogant sins (1 Corinthians 5:1-13)
   b. Undisciplined sins and dangerous influences upon the church (Acts. 5:1-10)
   c. Gossip (Ephesians 4:25)
   d. Murmuring (John 6:43 and 1 Corinthians 10:10)
   e. Talking behind a church leader's back in a negative way (Ephesians 4:28-29)
   f. Continuous non-support for church leadership (Ephesians 4:31)
   g. Openly out of fellowship with church, God, or a church member (Ephesians 4:26)
6. **Process for church discipline**
   a. Go privately and confront.
   b. If they will not listen, take one or two with you to confront.
   c. If they still will not listen, go to the church.
   d. If they will not repent, remove them from their responsibilities and possibly from church membership. (1 Corinthians 5:2-13, Titus 3:10, and 2 Thessalonians 3:14-15)
   e. If they repent, restore them to fellowship. The goal is for repentance and restoration to occur.[7]

Education

Learning Activity

1. How do you think a trained conflict management group in your church would be received?
2. What are some things you would be willing to do or get others to do in order to equip your congregation with conflict management?

Grandchild Story
(All you can eat or nothing)

William, our first grandson, was visiting us when we lived just five minutes from the Texas Rangers' ballpark. William had heard his school friends talk about the "all you can eat" section at the ballpark, so he asked if we could go to a Rangers' game and sit in that special section.

I told him we could get seats closer and as long as he was with me, he could eat all he wanted. William said he would rather sit in the "all you can eat" section. His father tried to explain to him that wherever he sat, if he was with Paw Paw, he could have all he wanted to eat. He was not convinced. We ended up sitting in the "all you can eat" section. We enjoyed the game and William enjoyed five hot dogs, two chicken sandwiches, and three big fountain drinks. He probably saved me money after all. Will is like many people I have known in conflict. They have their minds made up and cannot be changed.

Chapter 2

Mediation

The tasks of the mediator are as follows:

1. Facilitate a process and do not serve as judge.
2. Assist both parties in focusing on the issues.
3. Insist parties address each other and remind them not to look at or talk to the mediator.
4. Establish clear lines of communication.
5. Prioritize the values with both parties.
6. Resist overreacting and help the parties resist overreacting.
7. Be fair to both sides and keep the door open for future meetings if needed.

I. Mediation

A. Definition: Mediation is the art of listening and negotiating. Third party mediation is a process that provides structure and specific directions through which the church, groups, or individuals resolve their problems. Both parties must be willing to meet and commit to the process. A trained, skillful, spirit-filled mediator can keep many conflicts from escalating to a no–win situation. Mediation can be beneficial in the following:
   1. Member-member conflicts
   2. Member-pastor conflicts
   3. Staff-pastor conflicts

4. Staff-staff conflicts
5. Business meetings [1]

B. Descriptions from the Bible
1. Matthew 18:15-17

    "Moreover if thy brother shall trespass against thee, go and tell him his fault between thee and him alone: if he shall hear thee, thou hast gained thy brother. But if he will not hear thee, then take with thee one or two more, that in the mouth of two or three witnesses every word may be established. And if he shall neglect to hear them, tell it unto the church: but if he neglect to hear the church, let him be unto thee as an heathen man and a publican."

    Jesus commands third party mediation in conflict resolution.

2. Acts 6:1-8

    "And in those days, when the number of the disciples was multiplied, there arose a murmuring of the Grecians against the Hebrews, because their widows were neglected in the daily ministration. Then the twelve called the multitude of the disciples unto them, and said, It is not reason that we should leave the word of God, and serve tables. Wherefore, brethren, look ye out among you seven men of honest report, full of the Holy Ghost and wisdom, whom we may appoint over this business. But we will give ourselves continually to prayer, and to the ministry of the word. And the saying pleased the whole multitude: and they chose Stephen, a man full of faith and of the Holy Ghost, and Philip, and Prochorus, and Nicanor, and Timon, and Parmenas, and Nicolas a proselyte of Antioch: Whom they set before the apostles: and when they had prayed, they laid their hands on them. And the word of God increased; and the number of the disciples multiplied in Jerusalem greatly; and a great company of the priests were obedient to the faith. And Stephen, full of faith and power, did great wonders and miracles among the people."

    The early church leaders served as third party mediators.

3. Acts 15:1-35. Every time the church mediated a conflict and experienced resolution, the church grew.

C. **Description of a mediator**
   1. A spiritual person
      A mediator should not come across as a "Rambo"—a tough guy who forces his way—but rather as one who knows God and is in fellowship with God.
   2. A trusted person
      A mediator should reflect measurements of trust.
      Trust Measurements
      a. Flexible—able to adjust to various conflict management styles
      b. Fair—able to see that everyone has an opportunity to be heard and able to see all sides of an issue
      c. Firm–refuses to be manipulated
      d. Focused—constantly looking at the real issue and not becoming personal
      e. Full of Faith—has faith in God and in believers to resolve conflict
   3. A good communicator—A mediator should be a people-oriented person who quickly earns the respect of others.
   4. A facilitator—A mediator should be skilled in facilitating a process, not dictating the process. The process must be kept on track and not sabotaged.
   5. A resource person—a mediator must be able to suggest resources for each problem.
   6. A scapegoat—A mediator must be willing to absorb the anger of the conflicted parties in order to help bring about resolution.
   7. A moderator—When you are voted in by the church or empowered by the conflicted parties, you must be in charge. You must protect them from hurting each other.[2]

D. **Details of the Mediation Process** (See Conflict Management Diagnostic Points in Appendix A).
   1. Entry
      a. Someone from the church contacts you for help.
      b. Listen to the concerns.
      c. Explain the mediation process.
      d. Make it clear that you cannot help without being empowered by the pastor, church, and/or both conflicted parties.
      e. Clarify terms of Mediation Agreement.
      f. Arrange for a meeting.

g. At the meeting, explain the process again and have parties sign the Mediation Agreement.
2. Education
   a. Plan a training event, such as Conflict Management, with church leaders.
   b. Throughout the event, be constantly in the process of educating the parties on conflict management.
3. Enlightenment
   a. Request records, materials, demographics, constitution, and all other relevant documents.
   b. Possibly conduct a church-wide or leadership survey (Appendix C).
   c. Conduct individual and/or group interviews as it pertains to the conflict.
   d. Analyze the information.
   e. Report information to the party. You gain entry with confirmation and approval to continue.
4. Empower
   a. Decide who needs mediation and which type of mediation—church-wide, town hall meeting or only with parties involved in conflict. My experience suggests that the smaller the group, the more effective the mediation process. I suggest 2-4 from each side. Rarely does a church-wide, town hall meeting produce good results.
   b. Before meeting
      1) Agree on time and place, and sign the Medication Agreement.
      2) Arrange the room so that conflicted parties must face each other.
      3) Pray.
   c. Meeting
      1) Everyone greets each other.
      2) All present agree on ground rules.
         a) Allow only one person to talk at a time.
         b) Inform all present that each person will be respected and given equal opportunity to present his side.
         c) Disallow threats and ultimatums.
         d) Tell all present that talk in generalities is not acceptable. Each person must be specific with who said what, not "they said." Each person must give dates, places, and such.
         e) State that each person must be committed to a resolution.

> f) Explain that the process will continue until a reconciliation agreement is reached by all parties and recorded in writing.
> g) Instruct each person to deny self and submit to the leadership of Christ.
>
> 3) Mediator reads scripture on unity and reconciliation and leads in prayer. (Colossians 3:12-15; Romans 12:9-18, Ephesians 4:1-6, Philippians 4:4-9).
> 4) Each side shares the problem from their perspective.
> 5) Back and forth communication takes place.
> 6) Participants may brainstorm for a solution.
> 7) Mediator helps parties build on agreements and commitment for the future. If needed, another date is set to meet.
>
> 5. Reporting
>   a. Mediator reports to the party with whom he gained entry.
>   b. Mediator gives recommendations.
> 6. Resolution steps are implemented with mediation follow-up every three months for a year.[3]

E. Description of various mediation resources to aid in mediation.
The following are various mediation resources found in this book.
1. Mediation Agreement (See Appendix A)
2. Church Members Survey (See Appendix C)
3. Mediating Two Conflicted Parties
4. Mediating Staff Conflicts
5. Mediating a Business Meeting
6. Mediating Using the Gospel Approach

Two Conflicted Parties

What to do if approached by a person in church or by a pastor who shares with you a conflict that he/she is experiencing

Before Meeting

1. Ask if Matthew 18 has been followed. If not, ask them to follow Matthew 18 and return to you if no resolution is reached.
2. Ask them to read and sign the Mediation Agreement.
3. Ask for a room with chairs for all parties and 90 minutes without interruptions.
4. Ask God to give you wisdom.

During the Meeting

1. Everyone exchanges greetings
2. The mediator confirms that all agree on the ground rules (Mediation Agreement).
3. The mediator reads scripture on unity and reconciliation and leads in prayer. Scriptures suggested are Matthew 22:377-39, John 10:10, and 2 Corinthians 5:19
4. The mediator explains the process.
    A. The acronym given below will be used to conduct the process.
        Share scripture and prayer.
        Open with statements and rules.
        Listen to each side of the story.
        Verify what has been said.
        Explore various solutions leading to an agreement.
    B. The mediator will share the problem as he views it and give possible solutions. The mediator is not a judge but a facilitator of the mediation process.
    C. Dialogue for the purpose of arriving at agreed upon solution will take place. A written record will be kept and signed by both parties.
    D. If no agreement is reached, the mediator will determine if another meeting is needed or if there are other possible solutions.

Mediating Staff Conflict

What to do if approached by a pastor, church Personnel Committee, deacons, or staff member regarding a staff conflict.

Before Meeting

1. Ask if Matthew 18 has been followed. If not, ask them to follow Matthew 18 and return to you if no resolution is reached.
2. Ask them to sign the Covenant Agreement.
3. Ask them to read and sign the Mediation Agreement
4. Ask for a room with chairs for all parties and 90 minutes without interruptions. Arrange the chairs so conflicted parties face each other.
5. Ask for copies of job description, constitution and bylaws.
6. Ask God to give you wisdom.

During Meeting

1. Everyone exchanges greetings.
2. Parties agree on ground rules (Mediation Agreement).

3. The mediator reads scripture on unity and reconciliation and leads in prayer.
4. The mediator explains the three stages of this session.
   a. The story-telling stage.
      1) Each side is given ten minutes to talk.
      2) Each side is to tell their story uninterrupted.
   b. The problem-solving stage.
      1) Each side is given five minutes to concisely state the problem from their perspective.
      2) The mediator is to take 15 minutes to review the problem.
   c. The agreement stage.
      1) The mediator proposes an agreement in 5 minutes.
      2) Each side is given five minutes to respond.
      3) If a resolution is reached, a written record of the agreement is signed. If no agreement is reached, the mediator informs both sides that a report will be given to the pastor or appointed committee. If another meeting is necessary, the mediator will contact the parties.

Mediations

A Business Meeting

A church without a pastor

On occasion, a church without a pastor faces an issue, and members have little trust in the person serving as moderator. In these situations, a third party, outside mediator/moderator can help to insure fairness.

A church where the pastor's position is questioned or the pastor prefers not to moderate.

Under some circumstances, a church may experience a situation where members question the current pastor's leadership, or the issue is of such a nature that the pastor prefers not to serve as moderator. In these situations, a third party, outside mediator/moderator can help to ensure fairness.

A mediator/moderator who is asked to assist a church under these conditions should

1. be asked by the church to moderate by a majority vote.
2. be sensitive to the issue.

Mediation

3. be unbiased and fair to all concerned.
4. be firm in establishing authority and rules of conduct.
5. be committed to helping the church achieve unity.

Business Meeting-Rules of Conduct

You may be fully versed in Robert's Rules of Order of parliamentary procedure, but experience has taught me that the majority of people are not. In the spirit of fairness and to ensure the majority voice is heard, the following rules of conduct will be followed.

1. A motion is made that _____ serve as moderator. Someone seconds. Discussion is allowed. Vote is taken.
2. A motion is made that the printed rules of conduct be followed. Someone seconds. Discussion is allowed. Vote is taken.
3. A motion is made that the printed agenda be followed. Someone seconds. Discussion is allowed. Vote is taken. If this is a called meeting then only the issue for which the meeting was called can be considered. Thus no reports just the one item discussed.

Agenda for regular meeting	**Agenda for called meeting**
Call to Order (Moderator)	Call to Order (Moderator)
Season of Prayer	Season of Prayer
Minutes of previous meeting (Clerk)	Statement of purpose of meeting
Treasurer's Report (Treasurer)	Explain only the item(s) previously
Organization Reports	voted on can be discussed
Old Business	Read the motion
New Business	Discussion (alternate one for and one against)
Motion to Adjourn	Vote (Have printed ballots prepared)
	Have representative from each side count
	Announce results giving numbers
	Motion to Adjourn

Rules of Conduct

1. Motion on the floor.
   Any item for discussion must be started by a motion.
   Motions are made by raising your hand.
   Wait for the moderator to recognize you.
   Stand and begin by saying,
   "I move that _____."
   Wait for a second to the motion.
   Anyone can second by saying, "I second."
   Discussion.
   In discussion. . .
       only one at a time may speak.
       no one is to talk except the one speaking.
       no interruptions are allowed.
       one will speak *for* the motion.
       one will speak *against* the motion.
   After everyone has had time to speak for or against the motion. . .
2. The moderator asks, "Are you ready to vote?" The moderator will restate the motion and explain the method of voting (hands, voice, or secret ballot).
3. The vote is taken.
4. The vote is announced. (No verbal responses allowed.)
5. The purpose is to ensure that every voice who desires is heard and that everyone understands what they are voting on.

Other parliamentary procedures of *Robert's Rules of Order* will be allowed.

Learning Activity

1. Divide into groups and role-play a mediation situation.
2. Have two sides serve as conflicted parties and one person serve as a mediator.

Grandchild Story
(Expectations)

Grandchildren want to please their grandparents. One day when several grandchildren were visiting their grandmother's house, she gathered them all into a group and prepared to tell them a story.

"Now children, I want to tell you a story about someone who lives in the woods, but sometimes he comes into our yard. What is it?"

The grandchildren were silent. "Okay," grandmother said, "this creature has a bushy tail and likes to eat nuts. Now what do you think it is?"

Silence again. Grandmother said, "Let me try one more time. This creature lives in the woods, has a bushy tail, eats nuts, and climbs trees. Now what do you think it is?"

The oldest grandchild spoke up, "I know the answer you want is Jesus, but it sure sounds like a squirrel to me."

Chapter 3

Restoration

A. Restoration

1. Definition—Restoration is a ministry that gives care to someone who is hurt, wounded, broken, despised, fallen, and/or forsaken. Restoration ministry varies in its approach, method, contribution, and time. The goal is to restore the person to a right relationship with those concerned and to return the individual to useful service. Restoration is needed after a conflict for both the church as a whole and for the individuals who have experienced conflict. Restoration is a healthy process that takes time.
2. Description from the Bible—"Brethren, if a man is overtaken in any trespass, you who *are* spiritual restore such a one in a spirit of gentleness, considering yourself lest you also be tempted. Bear one another's burdens, and so fulfill the law of Christ" (NKJV).
3. Detail of Process – Restoration, by its very nature, cannot be programmatic but must be personal. The goal is to provide the following resources:
   a. Support Groups
      1) Establish support groups for both ministers and their wives.
      2) Ensure these groups are composed of those who have been hurt or terminated by their church.
   b. Supply the following resources to the churches.
      1.) Financial assistance to terminated ministers
      2.) Accountability group to assist in restoring a brother

3.) Professional counsel
4.) List of resources available from Association, State Convention, and Lifeway Resources, DiscipleGuide as well as community and para-church organizations
5.) Assistance in resume development and locating available church staff positions
6.) Barnabas House for free housing, food, and job placement until healed.

The Barnabas Ministry[1]

Mission

The Barnabas Ministry is based on the biblical person of Barnabas, whose name, according to Acts 4:36-37, means *encourager*. The Barnabas Ministry is a comprehensive, evolving ministry dedicated to providing encouragement and full restoration to hurting ministers.

Methodology

The Barnabas Ministry seeks full restoration for a wounded minister through a supporting church, employment, housing, accountability group, counseling, calling church, and covenant agreement.

Barnabas-Supporting Church

A Barnabas-supporting church will provide encouragement to a wounded minister and his family by providing:

1. A place to belong—When a minister and his family have been hurt, it is important for them to be able to move into a congregation that will love them and help them belong. The church as a whole will be encouraged to love the wounded minister's family, but a select group will be trained in administering acts of love.
2. A place to heal—When anyone has been hurt, he or she needs time to heal. Healing takes various forms and requires various lengths of time.
3. A place to go and grow—The primary concern of those who have experienced termination is, "Where will we go?" A primary need of those who have experienced termination is beginning a process of spiritual growth that culminates in full restoration.

Barnabas House

Employment will be twofold.

1. Secular employment—The wounded minister will be assisted in obtaining secular employment for 20-50 hours.
2. Church staff employment—The minister will be called to be on the staff of a church and/or association for 10-30 hours a week. This work will be in line with his gifts and calling. He may be asked to start a new Sunday School class, survey a new property development, file choral music, or other such activities.

Barnabas Accountability Group

The accountability group will function as mentors who will walk with the wounded minister and his family from beginning to end of this ministry. They will meet with him and his family at least weekly and become the wounded minister's advocate should any problems arise.

Barnabas Counseling

Professional counseling will be provided to the minister and his family on an approved schedule with the accountability group.

Barnabas Calling Church

The church is the next-place-of-service church for the minister. He will be briefed by the accountability group. After the minister has been called to the church, the accountability group will offer to work with the minister for up to 18 months.

Barnabas Covenant

The _____ Baptist Church and _____ Association of churches, desire to encourage ministers and their families who have experienced hurts such as forced termination. This is best accomplished when all parties have a clear understanding of the following **Covenant Agreement**.

General Conditions

1. The minister shall have been a pastor or ministerial staff member.
2. The minister shall have been referred to the church or church leader.

3. The church of the minister may terminate this Covenant Agreement at any time but must allow the minister 30 days to vacate the property upon written notice.

Minister's Commitment

1. The minister must disclose any current or anticipated legal actions, criminal or civil, and causes for termination as pertaining to himself or his family.
2. The minister must give written permission to a full background check for himself and any members of his family.
3. The length of the agreement shall be a maximum of one year.
4. The minister will contribute at least a tithe (10%) of his family income to the supporting church as well as be active in the ministry of the church.
5. The minister will fully cooperate with the Barnabas accountability group.

Church/Association Commitment

1. Love, encourage, pray for, and affirm the minister and family.
2. Provide pastoral care for the minister and family.
3. Provide Barnabas House, counseling, employment, and accountability group.

The Covenant Agreement is entered into voluntarily by the _____ Baptist Church, _____ Baptist Association and _____, Minster of the gospel, as witnessed by their signatures below.

_____   _____
Wounded Minister   Date

_____   _____
Church Clerk or Pastor   Date

_____   _____
Associational Moderator or Director   Date

Learning Activity

List ways you think your church could minister to another church leader in order to bring about restoration.

Summary of Section 3

1. **Education**—Conflict management is a continuous education process. A serious student of conflict management will read continuously on the subject and attend as many seminars on conflict as possible. Find your peers and learn from one another.
2. **Mediation**—Mediation is a process that will develop through years of experience. A person open to mediation ministry should develop a process and use it as much as possible, learning and improving as a mediator each time.
3. **Restoration**—There are numerous wounded ministers, ministers' wives, children, and church members. Some have made a decision to never attend church again. These wounded heroes of the faith need to be restored to active service.

I want to encourage pastors, deacons, and church leaders to equip themselves so they can help the hurting. This can be done by learning the Principles of Conflict, understanding what causes conflict by studying the top ten reasons for conflict, and preparing themselves to help resolve conflicts.

Principles of Conflict

1. Develop a definition of conflict.
2. Develop an understanding of conflict by studying the basic truths concerning conflict.
3. Be able to identify signs of conflict.
4. Understand the structural levels of conflict.

5. Be acquainted with various personality styles.

Understanding Causes of Conflict

1. Study the top ten causes of conflict.
2. Study how to avoid conflict.
3. Study how to bring about resolution.

Prepare Yourself to Help Resolve Conflict

1. Be a student of conflict management
2. Serve as a mediator of conflict
3. Share grace and help those who have been wounded by conflict

Conclusion

Conflict exists in churches and needs to be taken seriously. Churches should equip their members in conflict management. This can be achieved by teaching, preaching, holding seminars, and conducting special training sessions.

Proverbs 27:23 says, "Be sure you know the condition of your flocks, give careful attention to your herds;" (NIV).

Learning Activity

What is one thing you have read in this book that you think you can take away and use in your life and ministry?

Appendix A

Mediation Agreement

We, the undersigned parties, are presently involved in conflict with one another, and we hereby submit to the mediation process with an agreed upon mediator. We agree to follow the ground rules outlined in this agreement.

1. I agree that only one person will talk at a time.
2. I will respect and give the other side equal opportunity, seeking to understand before being understood.
3. I will not use threats or ultimatums.
4. I will not talk in generalities such as, "they said" but will use specifics, giving names, dates, and places to the best of my knowledge.
5. I agree to hold the mediator harmless for my observations, suggestions, or implications that said mediator may make in the course of mediation.
6. I waive any right of action that I may have against the mediator for any allegation of wrongful conduct or said mediator's part while acting in the course of the mediation herein agreed to.
7. I agree that the mediation is confidential and I will not call the mediators to serve as a witness to my case.
8. I will be committed to reconciliation.
9. The process will have a beginning and an ending, but I will continue the process until an agreement is reached by both parties.
10. I will deny self and submit to the leadership of Christ, agreeing to the following when needed:
    Apologize
    Accept an apology
    Accept the consequences
    Alter my behavior
    Ask for forgiveness
    Act upon the agreement

_____   _____   _____
     Party One   Party Two   Mediator

_____   _____   _____
    Church name   Pastor   Date

Appendix B

Conflict Settlement Agreement

We, the parties in this agreement, having participated in a mediation session(s) and being satisfied that we have reached a fair and reasonable settlement, hereby agree:

_____
_____
_____
_____
_____

We were unable to reach an agreement on the following issues, and they are not a part of our mediation agreement.

_____
_____
_____
_____
_____

We intend this document to be legally binding and an enforceable settlement.

Dated the _____ of _____
_____, 20_____

_____   _____
Signature of party one   Signature of party two

_____   _____
Witnessed by Mediator(s)

Appendix C

Church Member Survey

1. I have been a member of this church (check one)...

   _____ less than 1 year   _____ 5-10 years

   _____ 1-3 years   _____ 10-20 years

   _____ 3-5 years   _____ more than 20 years

2. I serve as (check all that apply)...

   _____ deacon   _____ Sunday School teacher

   _____ Sunday School worker   _____ committee chairperson

   _____ committee member   _____ choir member

   _____ mission organization   _____ other

Appendix C

3. How frequently do you attend?

	Sunday School	Morning Worship	Evening Worship	Wednesday Evening
Weekly				
3 x a month				
2 x a month				
1 x a month				
Occasionally				
Never				

4. What do you like best about your church?

5. Briefly state what you believe to be the church's greatest weakness.

6. If you could change one thing about this church, what would it be?

7. In terms of stress and intensity, mark your opinion of the present situation.

	1	2	3	4	5	6	7	8	9	10	
Harmonious											Conflict
Calm-happy											Crisis
United											Chaos

Appendix C

8. Describe briefly any concern/issue/conflict facing the church, as you understand it.

9. As it pertains to your answer in number 8. . .
   a. When do you think the problem began?
   b. What were some of the causes?
   c. What positive ideas do you have to solve it?

10. Who is the E. F. Hutton of your church (the person everyone listens to, respects, and has the most influence)?

11. Additional comments?

Appendix D

Entry	Who first made contact? Who are the conflicted parties? Have they attempted Matthew 18? Do they agree to the mediation process? Are they willing to sign the mediation agreement?

Enlightenment	Issues	Voiced problem Tacit problem
	Leaders	History of relationship Communication between
	Setting	Church size Church age Church location Church sociology Church growth/decline

Appendix D

Enlightenment
- Reason
  - Worship wars
  - Church polity
  - Staff
  - Sexual Immorality
  - Incompetence
  - Church conflicted
  - Communication
  - Change
  - Leadership
  - Control
- Level
  - Problem to solve
  - Disagreement
  - Contest
  - Fight/Flight
  - Intractable

Empower
- Strategies for management
- Education
- Mediation
- Restoration

Share scripture and prayer

Open with statement and rules

Listen to each side

Verify what has been said

Explore solutions leading to an agreement

End Notes

Section 1 Principles of Conflict, Introduction

[1] Michael Agnes. ed, *Webster's New World Dictionary and Thesaurus* (New York: Hungry Minds, 1996), 488.

Section 1, Chapter 1-Sentence Definitions of Conflict

[1] Agnes, 125.
[2] Larry McSwain and William C. Treadwell, Jr. *Conflict Ministry in the Church* (Nashville: Broadman Press, 1981), 25. Quote by Ross Stagner in *The Dimensions of Human Conflict*. Wayne State University Press, Detroit, 1967, p. 136. Also on *Church Fights, Managing Conflicts in the Local Church*, 28-29.
[3] Hugh F. Halverstadt. *Managing Church Conflict* (Louisville: Westminster John Knox Press, 1991), 4. Quoted from Morton Deutsch, "Conflicts: Productive and Destructive" reprinted in Fred Jandt, ed. *Conflict Resolution Through Communication*. (New York: Harper and Row, 1973), 156.
[4] Norman Shawchuck. *How to Manage Conflict in the Church: Understanding and Managing Conflict*, vol.1. (Leith, North Dakota: Spiritual Growth Resource Press), 35.
[5] Ken Sande. *The Peacemaker* (Grand Rapids: Baker Book House, 1991), 80.
[6] Sande. 83.
[7] Sande. 79-137.

End Notes

Section 1, Chapter 2-Scars from Conflict

[1] Marlin E. Thomas. *Resolving Disputes in Christian Groups* (Winnipeg Canada: Windflower Communications, 1994), 6.
[2] Jesse C. Fletcher. *The Southern Baptist Convention* (Nashville: Broadman & Holman Publishers, 1994), 39- 41.
[3] Harry Leon McBeth. *Texas Baptist* (Dallas, Texas: Baptist Way Press, 1998), 123.
[4] 2013-2014 *Directory and Handbook BMA America*, 53rd edition (Texarkana, Arkansas: Disciple Guide, 2013), 1.
[5] Gary Ledbetter. *The Day of Small Things* (Grapevine, Texas: Southern Baptists of Texas Convention, 2008), 92.
[6] *Reports from Director of Mission Surveys* (Nashville, Tennessee: Lifeway Christian Resources), Photocopied.
[7] G. Lloyd Rediger. *Clergy Killers* (Louisville: Westminster John Knox Press, 1997), 25.
[8] Norris Smith. "Conflict Management" (Glorieta, New Mexico: Church Leadership Week, July 3, 1999), Lecture, Handouts.
[9] Smith. Photocopied.

Section 1, Chapter 3-Sure Truths about Conflict-

[1] Smith. Photocopied.

Section 1, Chapter 4-Signs of Conflict

[1] Craig Webb. "Top 10 Predictable Times for Conflict in the Church," http://www.Lifeway.com/article/Top-Ten-Predictable-Times-for Conflict. Adapted from Speed Leas list in *Mastering Conflict and Controversy* by Edward G. Dobson and Marshall Shelley (Word Publishing, December 10, 1993).

Section 1, Chapter 5-Structural Levels of Conflict

[1] Speed Leas. *Moving Your Church Through Conflict* (Washington, S.C.: The Alban Institute, Inc., 1985), 17-23.

Section 1, Chapter 6-Styles of Conflict

[1] Tim LaHaye. *Spirit Controlled Temperament* (Wheaton, IL: Tyndale House Publishers, 1966), 8.
[2] LaHaye. 8.

³ Tancrede Wayman Flippin. *An Analysis of the Relationship Between Temperaments and Preferred Learning Styles of Students in Southern Baptist Seminaries. A Dissertation prospectus* (Louisville: The Southern Baptist Theological Seminary, 2000), 38.

⁴ Mels Carbonell. *Uniquely You in Christ* (Blue Ridge, GA: 1998), 7.

⁵ Ken Voges. *Adult DISC Survey* (Houston, Texas: In His Grace, Inc., 1995), 4.

⁶ Flippin. 2000, 40.

⁷ Ken Voges and Ron Braund. *Understanding How Others Misunderstand You* (Chicago, Ill.: Moody Press. 1990), 19-29.

⁸ William Smith. *A Comparative Analysis of Selected Pastors Personality Profiles and Their Conflict Management Styles. A Dissertation Prospectus* (Louisville: The Southern Baptist Theological Seminary, 2003), 73.

⁹ Ken Voges. *Team Building Survey* (Houston, Texas: In His Grace, Inc., 1995), 7.

Section 1, Chapter 7-Generational Differences

¹ Gary L. McIntosh. *One Church, Four Generation: Understanding and Reaching All Ages in Your Church* (Grand Rapids, Michigan: Baker Books Publishing, 2002), Summary.

Section 2 Problems (causes of conflict)

Section 2-Introduction

¹ *Survey's from Directors of Missions of the Southern Baptist Convention* (Nashville: Lifeway Christian Resources, 1984-2012), handouts.

² *Survey's from Directors of Missions of the Southern Baptist Convention*, handouts.

Section 2-Chapter 10- Worship Wars

¹ David Dykes. (September 3, 2006), "The Kind of Music God Loves," Sermon conducted from Green Acres Baptist Church, Tyler, Texas.

² Jack Taylor. *Hallelujah Factor* (Mansfield, PA: Kingdom Publishing, 1983), 172.

³ George Barna. "Focus on Worship Wars Hides the Real Issues Regarding Connection to God" (The Barna update http://www.barna.org. November 19, 2002).

⁴ Norris Smith. "Conflict Management" (Glorieta NM: Church Leadership Week, July 3, 1999), Lecture, Handout.

End Notes

Section 2-Chapter 9-Church Polity

¹ Chad Owen Brand and R. Staton Norman. *Perspectives on Church Government* (Nashville: Broadman and Holman, 2004), 1-25.
² Paul Engle, sr.ed., Steve Cowan, gen.ed., *Who Runs the Church?* (Grand Rapids, Michigan: Zondervan, 2004), 12-18.

Section 2-Chapter 8-Staff

¹ John McArthur, ed. *Pastoral Ministry* (Dallas, Texas: Thomas Nelson, 2005), 230-273.
² Jonamay Lambert and Selma Mayes. *50 Activities for Conflict Resolution*, (Amherst: MA. HRD Press. 1999), 7.

Section 2-Chapter 7-Sex

¹ Timothy Pect. "Wise up About Sex," www.Sermoncentral.
² Kent Hughes. *Sexual Immorality and Church Leaders*, www.GraceOnlineLibrary.
³ Centers for Disease Control and Prevention: "Morbidity and Mortality" *Weekly Report*, October 12, 2013.
⁴ Pect.
⁵ Baylor University, Clergy Sexual Misconduct Study, www.Baylor.Edu/clergy sexualmisconduct/index.

Section 2-Chapter 6-Incompetence

¹ David Dunning. "Thales Lament: Roadblocks on the Path to Knowing Thyself," (New York: Cornell University, April 13, 2000), http://www.thepsychologist.org.uk/archive/archive_home.cfm?volumeID=26&edition-ID=226&ArticleID=2282 (Sept. 21, 2013). Lecture.
² Rick Ezell. "Make No Excuses," www.lifeway.com, (July 11, 2012).
³ Bob Sheffield. *Avoid the Top Five Reasons for Pastor Termination, Part 3,* (June 12, 2008), http://www.lifeway.com.

Section 2-Chapter 5-Conflicted/Dysfunctional

¹ David Owens. *The Cure for Conflict*, www.sermoncentral.com.
² Ed Stetzer. "6 Signs Your Church is Dysfunctional." www.churchleaders.com/pastors/
³ D. G. McCoury. *Lecture on Single Staff Church,* (Double Mountain Baptist Area, Stanford, Texas, 1989), Notes.

Section 2-Chapter 4-Communication

¹ Dean Courtier. *Communication or Miscommunication*, www.sermoncentral.com, (February 21, 2010).
² Courtier.
³ David Dykes. "The Three Laws of Personal Communication." Green Acres Baptist Church, Tyler, Texas. (May 2002), Sermon.
⁴ Lambert and Myers. 27-28.

Section 2-Chapter 3-Change

¹ Chris Kelly, Chris. "How to Deal with Life's Greatest Changes," www.sermoncentral.com. (August 6, 2000).
² Greg Yount. "How Do You Feel About Change." www.sermoncentral.com.
³ Arnold L. Cook. *Historical Drift.* (Camp Hill, Pennsylvania: Christian Publication, 2000). xiii.
⁴ Bob Sheffield. "Avoid the Top Five Reasons for Pastoral Termination." http://www.lifeway.com. (June 23, 2008).
⁵ Norris Smith. "Why People Resist Chang." (Nashville: Lifeway Christian Resources, 2000), Lecture.
⁶ Lambert and Myers. 31.

Section 2-Chapter 2-Leadership Too Strong/ Leadership Too Weak

¹ Alex D. Montoya. "Leading." *Pastoral Ministry.* John MacArthur, ed., (Dallas, Texas: Thomas Nelson, 2005), 281.

Section 2-Chapter 1-Control

¹ *Surveys from Director of Missions*, 1984-2012.
² Kenneth C. Haugh. *Antagonists in the Church* (Minneapolis: Augsburg Publishing House, 1988), 25-30.
³ G. Lloyd Rediger. *Clergy Killers* (Louisville: Westminster. John Know Press, 1997), 25.

Section 2-Summary

¹ Francis Frangipane. *It's Time to End Church Splits*, (Cedar Rapids, IA: Arrow Publications, 2002), 4.
² Frangipane.

Section 3 Possibilities (cures for Conflict)

Section 3-Introduction

[1] Ken Sande and Ted Kober. *Guiding People Through Conflict* (Billings, Montana: Peacemaker Ministries, 1998), 5-17.

Section 3-Education

[1] Norris Smith, *Church Conflict Mediation Seminar* (Nashville, TN: Church Program Training Center, 1995), Notes.
[2] Smith, Notes
[3] Smith, Notes
[4] John Drakeford. *The Awesome Power of the Listening Ear*. (Waco, Texas: Word Book, 1973).
[5] Sande. *The Peacemaker*, 207.
[6] Sande. 137.
[7] Sande. 192-196.

Section 3-Mediation

[1] Richard Blackburn and Robert Williamson. *Facilitating Healthy Pastor Congregation Relations*. (Lombard, Illinois: Lombard Mennonite Peace Center, 1999), 3-7.
[2] Ken Coffee. *A Mediation Process*, Lecture conducted from the (Baptist General Convention of Texas in Dallas, Texas, 2000), Lecture. 6-8 handouts.
[3] Smith, Notes.

Section 3-Restoration

[1] Bob Anderson. Report of the Ministry of Antioch Affection. (Tuscawilla, Florida, 2000), Report conducted from the Pastor's Conference of the Dogwood Trails Baptist Area in Jacksonville, Texas, photocopied.

References

Agnes, Michael. *Webster New World Dictionary.* New York: Hungry Minds, 1996. Print.

Anderson, Bob. "Report of the Ministry of Antioch Affection." Pastor's Conference. Dogwood Trails Area. Jacksonville, TX. 2000. Lecture.

Augsburger, David. *Caring Enough to Confront.* Ventura: Regal Books, 1981. Print.

Barna, George. "Focus on Worship Wars Hides the Real Issues Regarding Connection to God." *The Barna Update.* N.p., 19 Nov. 2002. Web. 26 Nov 2013.< http://www.barna.org>.

Blackaby, Henry, and Richard Blackaby. *Spiritual Leadership.* Nashville: Broadman& Holman, 2001. Print.

—. "Clergy Sexual Misconduct Study." Baylor University. Web. 1 Oct. 2013. <www.Baylor.edu/clergysexualmisconduct>.

Blackburn, Richard, and Robert Williamson. "Facilitating Healthy Pastor Congregation Relations." Lombard: Lombard Mennonite Peace Center, 1999.

Brand, Chad Owen, and R. Stanton Norman. *Perspectives on Church Government.* Nashville: Broadman & Holman, 2004. Print.

Butts, Thomas Lane. "The Consequences of Miscommu-nication." N.p., 10 Dec. 2009. Web. 1 Oct. 2013. <www.day1.org/1723-dr-thomas-lane-butts-the-consequences-of-miscommunication>.

Carbonell, Mels. *Uniquely You in Christ.* Blue Ridge: Uniquely You, 1998. Print.

Coats, Darrell. "A Change in Leadership." SermonCentral, June 2009. Web. 10, Oct. 2013. <www.sermoncentral.com>.

References

Coffee, Ken. "A Mediation Process." Baptist General Convention of Texas. BGCT. Dallas. 2000. Keynote Address.

Coffee, Blake. *Unity Facilitator*. Dallas: Texas Baptist Leadership Center, Inc., of Baptist General Convention of Texas, 1998. Print.

Courtier, Dean. "Communication or Miscommunication." SermonCentral, Sept. 2010. Web. <www.sermoncentral.com>.

Covey, Stephen. *The 7 Habits of Highly Effective People*. New York: Fireside Book, 1989. Print.

Dale, Robert. *To Dream Again: How to Help Your Church Come Alive*. Nashville: Broadman Press, 1997. Print.

Dobson, Edward G., Speed Leas, and Marshall Shelley. *Mastering Conflict and Controversy*. Portland: Multnomah, 1992. Print.

Dunavant, Donald R. *Growing Churches*. 1996. Print.

Dunning, David. "Survey." New York Cornell University. N.p., n.d. Web. Oct. 15, 2013. <www.preaching today.com>.

Dykes, David. "The Three Laws of Personal Communication." Green Acres Baptist Church. Tyler, Texas. 19 May 2002. Lecture.

Dykes, David. "The Kind of Music God Loves." Green Acres Baptist Church. Tyler, Texas. 3 Sept. 2006. Sermon.

Engle, Paul and Steve Cowan, ed., *Who Runs the Church*. Grand Rapids: Zondervan, 2004. Print

Ezell, Rick. "Make No Excuses." Lifeway. 11 Jul 2012. Web. 10, Oct. 2013. <www.lifeway.com>.

Ferrell, Nancy K. "Conflict Resolution and Mediation Training." Conflict Resolution and Mediation Training. Baptist General Convention of Texas. Dallas. 1995. Keynote Address.

Fletcher, Jesse C. *The Southern Baptist Convention*. Nashville: Broadman & Holman, 1994. Print.

Flippin, Tancrede W. An Analysis of the Relationship Between Temperaments and Preferred Learning Styles of Students in Southern Baptist Seminaries. Diss. The Southern Baptist Theological Seminary, 2000. Louisville: The Southern Baptist Theological Seminary, Print.

Frangipane, Francis. *It's Time to End Church Splits*. Cedar Rapids: Arrow Publications, 2002. Print.

Gangel, Kenneth O., and Samuel L. Canine. *Communication and Conflict Management*. Nashville: Broadman, 1992. Print.

Halverstadt, Hugh. *Managing Church Conflict*. Louisville: Westminster John Knox, 1991. Print.

Hamric, Jeff. "What is a Pastor?." SermonCentral. Apr. 1994. Web. 23 Oct. 2013. <www.sermoncentral.com>.

Haugk, Kenneth C. *Antagonists in the Church*. Minneapolis: Augsburg, 1998. Print.

References

Hayes, Kenneth E. "Survey to Learn How to Resolve Conflict." Nashville: BSSB Research Department, 1990. Print.

Haynes, Michael. "Deacons as Agents of Change." *The Deacon*, 2002: 9-11. Print.

Hughes, Kent. "Sexual Immorality and Church Leaders." Grace Online Library. n.d. Web. 23 Oct. 2013. <www.graceonlinelibrary>.

Keirsey, David. *Please Understand Me II*. Delmar: Prometheus Nemesis,1998. Print.

Kelly, Chris. "How to Deal with Life's Greatest Changes." SermonCentral. Aug. 2000. Web. 24 Oct. 2013. <www.sermoncentral.com>.

LaHaye, Tim. *Spirit-Controlled Temperament*. Wheaton: Tyndale, 1966. Print.

Lawson, Linda. "You're Fired!" *Church Administration*. 26 Jul. 2010: 3-8. Print.

Leas, Speed. *Discover Your Conflict Management Style*. Washington D. C.: The Alban Institute, 1984. Print.

—. *Moving Your Church Through Conflict*. Washington D. C.: The Alban Institute, 1985. Print.

Ledbetter, Gary. *The Day of Small Things: A History of the Southern Baptist of Texas Convention, 1998-2008*. Grapevine, Tx: Southern Baptists of Texas Convention, 2008. Print.

Lewis, Douglas. *Resolving Church Conflicts*. San Francisco: Harper, 1981. Print.

Littauer, Florence. *How to Get Along with Difficult People*. Eugene: Harvest House, 1984. Print.

London, Jr., H. B., and Neil B. Wiseman. *Pastors at Risk*. Wheaton: Victor Books, 1993. Print.

—. *Your Pastor is an Endangered Species*. Wheaton: Victor Books, 1996. Print.

Mains, David R. *Healing the Dysfunctional Church Family*. Wheaton: Victor Books, 1992 Print.

Marion, Lucille Ann. Conflict Management and Personality Types Among Community College Executives. Diss. Abstract. State U of New York at Albany, 1995. Print.

Maxwell, John C. *The 21 Irrefutable Laws of Leadership*. Nashville: Thomas Nelson, 1998. Print.

McBeth, Leon. *Texas Baptist*. Dallas: Baptist Way Press, 1998. Print.

McCoury, D. G. *Understanding the Single Staff Church*. Nashville: Convention Press, 1988. Print.

—. *Pastoring the Single Staff Church*. Nashville: Convention Press, 1990. Print.

—. "Single Staff Church." Stanford: Double Mountain Baptist Area, 1989. Photocopied lecture.

References

McIntosh, Gary L. *One Church, Four Generation: Understanding and Reaching All Ages in Your Church.* Grand Rapids: Baker Books, 2002. Print.

McSwain, Larry L., and William C. Treadwell, Jr. *Conflict Ministry in the Church.* Nashville: Broadman, 1981. Print.

Mims, George. *The 7 Churches Not in the Book of Revelation.* Nashville: Holman, 2001. Print.

Montoya, Alex D. "Leading." *Pastoral Ministry.* John MacArthur, ed., Dallas: Thomas Nelson, 2005, 281. Print.

Owens, David. "The Cure for Conflict." SermonCentral. July 2006. Web. 1 Nov. 2013. <www.sermoncentral.com>.

Parson, George. *Intervening in a Church Fight: A Manual for Internal Consultants.* Washington D. C.: The Alban Institute,1989. Print.

Pect, Timothy. "Wise Up About Sex." SermonCentral. April 2002. Web. 8 Nov 2013. <www.sermoncentral.com>.

Powell, Paul W. *Basic Bible Sermons on Handling Conflict.* Nashville: Broadman. 1992. Print.

—. *Getting the Lead Out of Leadership.* Nashvill: Broadman. 1997. Print.

Rediger, Lloyd G. *Clergy Killers.* Louisville: Westminster, 1997. Print.

Reports from the Director of Missions Surveys. Nashville: Lifeway Christian Resources, 2012. Photocopied.

Sande, Ken. *The Peacemaker.* Grand Rapids: Baker Book House, 1991 Print.

Sande, Ken, and Ted Tobler. *Guiding People Through Conflict.* Billings: Peacemaker Ministries, 1998. Print.

Santrock, John W. *Psychology: The Science of Mind and Behavior.* Dubuque: W.M.C. Brown, 1986. Print.

Savage, John. "Conflict Management and Congregational Corporate Pain." Conflict Management and Congregational Corporate Pain Workshop. Reynoldsburg, Ohio. 1999. Keynote Address.

Schaller, Lyle E. *The Interventionist.* Nashville: Abingdon, 1997. Print.

Shawchurch, Norman. *How to Manage Conflict in the Church.* Leith: Spiritual Growth Resources, 1983. Print.

Shelley, Marshall. *Well-Intentioned Dragons.* Waco: Word Books, 1985. Print.

Sheffield, Bob. "Avoid the Top Five Reasons for Pastor Termination." Part 2 *Lifeway.* 12 Jun 2008. Web. 15 Nov 2013. <http://www.lifeway.com>.

—. "Avoid the Top Five Reasons for Pastor Termination." Part 3. *Lifeway.* 23 Jun 2008. Web. 15 Nov 2013. <http://www.lifeway.com>.

—. "Avoid the Top Five Reasons for Pastor Termination." Part 1. *Lifeway.* 7 Jun 2008. Web. 15 Nov 2013. <http://www.lifeway.com>.

Smith, Norris. "Church Conflict Mediation." Church Conflict Mediation Seminar. The Sunday School Board of The Southern Baptist Convention. Nashville, TN. 1995. Keynote Address. Photocopied.

References

Smith, Norris. "Lectures on Conflict Mediation." Church Leadership Week. Glorieta, NM. 3 July 1999. Keynote Address. Photocopied.

Smith, William. "A Comparative Analysis of Selected Pastors Personality Profiles and Their Conflict Management Styles." Diss. Southern Baptist Theological Seminary, 2003. Print.

Stienke, Peter L. How Your Church Family Works. Washington D. C.: Alban Institute, 1993. Print.

—. "Surveys from Directors of Missions of the Southern Baptist Convention." Nashville, TN: Lifeway Christian Resources, 1984-2012. Handout.

Taylor, Jack. Hallelujah Factor. Mansfield: Kingdom Publishing, 1983. Print.

Taylor, Robert M.. Taylor-Johnson Temperament Analysis Handbook. Los Angeles: Psychological Publications, 1984. Print.

Thomas, Marlin E.. Resolving Disputes in Christian Groups. Winnipeg: Windflower Communications, 1994. Print.

Thompson, Carolyn B., and James W. Ware. The Leadership Genius of George W. Bush. Hoboken: Wiley and Sons, 2003. Print.

Voges, Ken. Adult DISC Survey. Houston: In His Grace, 1997. Print.

—. Team Building Survey. Houston: In His Grace, 1995. Print.

Voges, Ken, and Ron Braund. Understanding How Others Misunderstand You. Chicago: Moody Press, 1990. Print.

Voges, Ken, and Mike Kempainen. Discovering the Leadership Styles of Jesus. Houston: In His Grace, 2001. Print.

Webb, Craig. Lifeway. N.p. Web. 7 Nov 2013. <http://www.Lifeway.com>.

Webb, Richard Bruce. A Practical Guide to Equipping Church Leadership with Conflict Management Skills. D. Min. project. Southwestern Baptist Theological Seminary, 1995. Print.

Weiten, Wayne. Psychology Applied to Modern Life. 2nd. ed. Monterrey, CA: brooks/Coke Publishing Company, 1986. Print.

Williamson, Charles Lee, and Margaret McCommon-Dempsey. Growing Your Church in Seven Days. Dallas, TX: Creative Church Consultations, Inc., 1994. Print.

Yount, Greg. "How Do You Feel About Change?" Sermon Central. N.p., n.d. Web. 2 Nov 2013. <www.sermoncentral.com>.

—. 2013-2014 Baptist Missionary Association Directory and Handbook. 53rd. ed. Texarkana, AR: Disciple Guide, 2013. Print.

CPSIA information can be obtained at www.ICGtesting.com
Printed in the USA
LVOW03s1735240414

383084LV00001B/1/P